vegetarian food for friends

simply spectacular recipes

vegetarian food for friends

simply spectacular recipes

Jane Noraika

with photography by **william lingwood**

RYLAND
PETERS
& SMALL

LONDON NEW YORK

Dedication

Mum, with love and thanks

Originally published as *New Vegetarian Entertaining* in Great Britain in 2003

This paperback edition published in 2007
by Ryland Peters & Small
20–21 Jockey's Fields
London WC1R 4BW
www.rylandpeters.com

Text © Jane Noraika 2003, 2007
Design and photographs
© Ryland Peters & Small 2003, 2007

10 9 8 7 6 5 4 3 2 1

ISBN 978-1-84597-390-2

A catalogue record for this book is available from the British Library.

Printed and bound in China.

Commissioning Editor
Elsa Petersen-Schepelern
Editor
Kim Davies
Production
Patricia Harrington
Art Director
Gabriella Le Grazie
Publishing Director
Alison Starling

Food Stylist
Joss Herd
Stylist
Antonia Gaunt
Indexer
Hilary Bird
Photographer's Assistant
Emma Bentham-Wood

NOTES

All spoon measurements are level unless otherwise stated.

All eggs are medium unless otherwise stated.

All fruits and vegetables should be washed thoroughly and peeled, unless otherwise stated. Unwaxed citrus fruits should be used whenever the zest will be used. When unavailable, the fruit should be washed in warm water.

Barbecues, ovens and grills should be preheated to the required temperature – if using a fan-assisted oven, cooking times should be reduced according to the manufacturer's instructions.

Specialist Asian ingredients are available in large supermarkets, Thai and Chinese shops, as well as in Asian stores.

Author's Acknowledgements

I would like to thank everyone who made the experience of producing this book so rewarding, satisfying and, in particular, fun. I would like to single out Mel Barrett for her enthusiasm and ideas whilst testing some recipes with me, particularly on the Sunday lunch section. Also Gabi Matzeu for sharing a few of his family's Italian secrets. A big thank you to Joss and William for working their magic on creating and photographing the food. It was a pleasure to share my house for 10 days with them when they were doing this. A big thank you to everyone at Ryland Peters and Small.

contents

introduction

Oh the joys of cooking! Everywhere we go or wherever we look, our taste-buds are bombarded by images of food. There they are on TV showing us how to produce a three-course meal at supersonic speed, and in magazine or newspaper articles instructing us on what we should be eating, how to cook it and, what's more, which 'trendy' ingredients we should be using. We are further seduced by the wondrous array of materials available in supermarkets, specialized shops and delicatessens. Never before has there been so much pressure on the cook to produce amazing varied food, effortlessly and joyfully. And then a vegetarian shows up ...

You are already pushed to your limit on time and creative ability, and feel that the evening is going to be spent in lonely solitude in the kitchen with only the oven as company.

My aim with *New Vegetarian Entertaining* is for you to take a sigh of relief and relax. It is possible to produce amazing food, even for a lot of people, and spend time with those you really want to – your guests. As the host, the objective is to do as much as possible in advance, taking any last-minute strain out of the occasion and making sure that your guests are greeted by the aromas of beautiful home-cooked food when they arrive.

There are chapters in this book on various social settings with dishes to suit each one. When your vegetarian friend appears, rather than your heart sinking, it should be a time to impress all your guests, whether they're vegetarian or not. When I cater for large private parties, I love it when a guest comments, in surprise, at the end of the party that they didn't even notice that no meat was used. Vegetarian food has long come out of the wilderness years of nut roasts and cutlets. Now, more than ever, with the multitude of cosmopolitan ingredients at our disposal, plus organic produce and farmers' markets springing up everywhere, it is possible to produce modern, clean-tasting food that is both easy on the eye and that will sit effortlessly alongside meat and fish, allowing vegetarians to blend in with the crowd.

FINGERFOOD

herb and feta polenta

topped with sun-dried tomato tapenade

These polenta rounds are a dream for any party because everything can be made in advance – in fact, if you are super-organized you can make the tapenade several weeks ahead. When serving polenta firm, it is always better to leave it overnight to set. You can cut it up and top with the tapenade a few hours before the party. Bring out the colours by serving on a bed of green leaves such as lamb's lettuce, rocket or watercress.

30 g unsalted butter

1 tablespoon olive oil

1 garlic clove, crushed

3 spring onions, finely chopped

50 g polenta

100 g feta cheese, crumbled into small pieces

a small handful of dill, coarsely chopped

sea salt and freshly ground black pepper

8–16 pitted black olives, sliced, to serve

TOMATO TAPENADE

50 g sun-dried tomatoes, soaked overnight in warm water with 1 tablespoon vinegar

6 tablespoons olive oil

1 tablespoon balsamic vinegar

1/2 red chilli, deseeded

a small handful of basil leaves

a baking tin, 20 cm square, well greased

a biscuit cutter, 5 cm diameter

MAKES 16

To make the tapenade, put the soaked tomatoes in a blender with the olive oil, balsamic vinegar, chilli and basil. Process until fairly smooth.

To make the polenta, put the butter, oil, garlic and spring onions in a saucepan and cook for 10 minutes until the onions are translucent. Pour in 300 ml boiling water, then add the polenta in a steady stream, whisking all the time to stop lumps forming. Continue cooking according to the instructions on the polenta packet. Stir in the feta and dill, add salt and pepper to taste, then pour into the prepared tin. Chill in the refrigerator overnight.

Cut out 16 small rounds with the biscuit cutter. Top each round with a generous spoonful of tapenade and a few sliced black olives, then serve.

COOK'S TIP

To store the tapenade, put in a screw-top jar and cover with a thin layer of olive oil. Keep in the refrigerator for 2–3 weeks. The tapenade also makes a good crostini topping or a pasta sauce.

1 baguette, thinly sliced

olive oil, for brushing

GUACAMOLE

2 ripe avocados, peeled and stones removed

1 tomato, quartered, deseeded and finely chopped

1/2 red onion, very finely chopped

freshly squeezed juice of 1 lime

1/2 garlic clove, crushed

1 teaspoon olive oil

sea salt and freshly ground black pepper

fresh coriander, coarsely chopped, to serve

a baking tray

MAKES 12

crostini with guacamole

There are lots of different tricks used to prevent avocado from discolouring. Some of the more successful ones are to use citrus juice, to cover the bowl with clingfilm, or to leave an avocado stone in the guacamole until you are ready to serve. To make absolutely sure of a good colour, avoid making the dip too far in advance, and if possible serve it as soon as it's made. That shouldn't be difficult – this dish is hard to resist!

Brush both sides of the bread with olive oil and put on the baking tray. Toast in a preheated oven at 200°C (400°F) Gas 6 for 5 minutes on each side until crisp and lightly golden.

Meanwhile, to make the guacamole, put the avocado in a bowl and mash with a fork until fairly smooth. Stir in the tomato, red onion, lime juice, garlic and olive oil. Add salt and pepper to taste.

Top each toasted slice with a generous spoonful of guacamole, then serve with coriander on top.

baby tomatoes
filled with pesto risotto

Be warned, if you are using cherry tomatoes this can be fiddly and a little time-consuming. However, I have made them for seventy and survived! When using larger tomatoes, provide your guests with plates or be prepared for a major clean-up operation. For a hassle-free approach, make the risotto and scoop out the insides of the tomatoes a day ahead, then fill them before your guests arrive. This dish is well worth the trouble, and the combination of tomato and basil is always a big hit.

Using a small, sharp knife, slice off the stalk end of each tomato and reserve. To make sure the tomatoes sit squarely on a plate, slice off the pointed bases. Using a teaspoon, scoop out the insides and turn upside-down to drain out any excess juices.

Melt the butter in a saucepan, then add the olive oil and garlic. Add the onion and cook for 10 minutes until softened. Add the rice, stirring to absorb the buttery juices. Add the stock a ladle at a time, stirring frequently and letting the rice absorb the liquid between each addition – about 15 minutes. Stir in the pesto, add salt and pepper to taste, then let cool.

Using a teaspoon, fill each tomato with risotto. Press the reserved lids on top at a jaunty angle, then serve.

16 baby tomatoes, preferably on the vine

25 g unsalted butter

1 tablespoon olive oil

1 garlic clove, crushed

1/2 white onion, finely chopped

70 g risotto rice, such as arborio

300 ml vegetable stock or hot water

1 tablespoon pesto

sea salt and freshly ground black pepper

MAKES 16

garlic croutons

with camembert and caramelized onion

A sophisticated French take on the very popular cheese on toast!

1 baguette, thinly sliced

1 tablespoon olive oil, plus extra for brushing

1 garlic clove

1 onion, quartered, then thinly sliced

1 teaspoon brown sugar

a pinch of salt

100 g Camembert cheese, thinly sliced

sprigs of thyme, to serve

a baking tray

MAKES 12

Put the slices of bread on the baking tray and lightly brush each side with olive oil. Toast in a preheated oven at 200°C (400°F) Gas 6 until both sides are lightly golden. Rub the garlic clove over one or both sides of the toast, depending on how much you love garlic.

Meanwhile, heat the 1 tablespoon oil in a saucepan, add the onion and cook gently for 10 minutes until softened. Stir in the sugar and a pinch of salt.

Put a thin slice of Camembert on each crouton, then pile the onion mixture on top. Serve topped with a tiny sprig of thyme.

COOK'S TIP

I love the flavour of garlic, but it can easily dominate a dish if you use too much. A good rule to remember is that the less garlic is cut or crushed, the stronger the flavour will be. In this recipe a whole uncut clove is being rubbed over the toast, so moderation is required.

tandoori tofu

These succulent, spicy morsels are original enough to surprise any guest. Be sure to make plenty of them since they make for very compulsive eating. They go brilliantly with drinks.

Cut the tofu into bite-sized pieces and put into a large bowl.

Put the yoghurt into another bowl, add the tomato purée, garlic, ginger, chilli, salt and toasted cumin and coriander seeds, and stir well. Spoon the mixture over the tofu and toss gently so that each piece is well coated. Set aside to marinate in the refrigerator for at least 1 hour.

Spread over a baking tray and cook in a preheated oven at 200°C (400°F) Gas 6 for 40 minutes, stirring halfway through the cooking time.

Transfer to a platter, then sprinkle with the lemon juice and coriander.

Let your guests help themselves to these succulent pieces of tofu, using a cocktail stick. Alternatively, thread a tiny wedge of lemon onto each stick, followed by a tofu cube.

COOK'S TIPS

The best way to store fresh ginger is in the freezer. Using a fine grater, grate as much of the frozen ginger as you need with no peeling or waste.

To be super-organized, marinate the tofu overnight in the refrigerator.

600 g deep-fried tofu

150 g thick plain yoghurt

2 tablespoons tomato purée

1 garlic clove, crushed

3 cm fresh ginger, grated

1 green chilli, finely chopped including seeds

1 teaspoon salt

1 teaspoon cumin seeds, lightly toasted in a dry frying pan and ground in a coffee grinder

2 teaspoons coriander seeds, lightly toasted in a dry frying pan and ground in a coffee grinder

freshly squeezed juice of $1/2$ lemon

fresh coriander, coarsely chopped, to serve

a baking tray

cocktail sticks

MAKES ABOUT 12

smoky spanish tortilla

375 g potatoes

1 tablespoon olive oil

7 spring onions, thinly sliced

⅓ teaspoon Spanish smoked paprika

1 garlic clove, crushed

½ red chilli, deseeded and finely chopped

6 eggs, lightly beaten

sea salt and freshly ground black pepper

a non-stick frying pan, 22 cm diameter

MAKES ABOUT 30

This delicious variation of the classic Spanish omelette includes the rather potent addition of smoked paprika. It works well as part of a fingerfood selection because it's fairly filling – and so helps prevent your guests from getting too merry too quickly! For the best results, make it on the same day as you are going to serve it. This tortilla also makes a delicious rustic lunch – try it sandwiched between two pieces of crusty bread with just a little mayonnaise.

Cook the potatoes for 15 minutes in plenty of boiling, salted water. When tender, drain through a colander and let cool before cutting into small chunks.

Put the oil in the frying pan. Add the spring onions, paprika, garlic and chilli and cook for 5 minutes until the onion has softened.

Add salt and pepper to the beaten eggs, then stir in the cooked potatoes. Add the mixture to the pan. Keep the eggs moving in the pan until they start to set, then continue to cook the tortilla for a few more minutes, keeping the heat low. Invert the tortilla onto a plate, then slide back into the pan, uncooked side down. Cook for a further 3–4 minutes before sliding onto a plate (the centre of the tortilla should still be a little soft).

Let cool slightly, then cut into about 30 diamond-shaped pieces or serve in larger wedges.

COOK'S TIP

Add some spinach, black olives and freshly chopped dill for a Greek-style tortilla.

pumpernickel squares
with cream cheese, horseradish and beetroot

People either love or hate beetroot – I definitely fall into the 'love it' category. I enjoy making these delicious bites because they look divine. When preparing fingerfood, the aesthetics are very important, and beetroot lends its magnificent colour. You may even recruit a few converts along the way!

150 g cream cheese

3 teaspoons horseradish

250 g (about 6 slices) pumpernickel, each slice cut into 4 squares

75 g cooked beetroot (with no vinegar), sliced thinly into rounds

4 gherkins, thinly sliced

2 hard-boiled eggs, finely chopped

fresh dill, coarsely chopped, to serve

MAKES ABOUT 24

Mix the cream cheese and horseradish in a bowl, then spread over the squares of pumpernickel. Top with a slice of beetroot, then a slice of gherkin, some chopped hard-boiled egg and fresh dill.

COOK'S TIPS

Use squares of rye toast instead of pumpernickel.

Roast some halved walnuts with a little cayenne pepper and soy sauce. Let cool, then use to top the beetroot – omit the gherkin and egg. Finish with a thin slice of apple.

wild mushroom and almond moneybags

Creamy-textured ground almonds are a wonderful alternative to the less exciting breadcrumbs that are often used to stuff mushrooms. The slight sweetness of the almonds is a magnificent complement to the rich meatiness of wild mushrooms.

1 tablespoon olive oil, plus extra for brushing

½ teaspoon paprika

500 g mixed mushrooms, thinly sliced

3 spring onions, finely chopped

a bunch of flat leaf parsley, finely chopped

2 tablespoons ground almonds

1 teaspoon lemon juice

sea salt and freshly ground black pepper

200 g filo pastry, thawed if frozen

a baking tray, lightly greased

MAKES 8

Put the olive oil, paprika, mushrooms and spring onions in a large frying pan, then cook for 10–15 minutes until the mushrooms are tender and start to release their liquid. Stir in the parsley, ground almonds, lemon juice, salt and pepper.

If the filo pastry isn't already rolled, roll it out to about 3 cm thick. Cut the pastry into 15 cm squares. Keeping the others covered with a damp cloth while you work, put a sheet of filo on a work surface and brush lightly with olive oil. Put another square of filo on top and lightly brush again with oil.

Put a spoonful of mushroom mixture in the centre. Pull the edges of the filo up to the middle, twist to seal, then put on the prepared baking tray. Repeat to make 8 moneybags.

Bake in a preheated oven at 180°C (350°F) Gas 4 for 20 minutes until lightly golden brown (if the tops brown too quickly, cover loosely with foil to stop them burning).

COOK'S TIPS

For a great main course, make larger moneybags and serve with roasted tomatoes and a selection of vegetables.

If you can't find ground almonds in the baking section of the supermarket, use flaked almonds and grind them yourself using a small blender or a mortar and pestle.

roasted red pepper and goats' cheese rolls

These rolls are a fabulous addition to any array of fingerfood. They may seem slightly complicated, but there are many ways to make life simpler: buy the tapenade or make it up a couple of weeks in advance, roast and peel the peppers the night before, then assemble the rolls well in advance. These are a real treat for the taste-buds, with sweet, tart and salty flavours in one mouthful. The vibrant red of the pepper is also very alluring.

Put the peppers on the baking tray and sprinkle with olive oil. Roast in a preheated oven at 220°C (425°F) Gas 7 for about 30 minutes until charred and blistered. Remove from the oven and cover with a damp tea towel. Set aside for 5–10 minutes to steam off the skins – this makes peeling much easier.

Meanwhile, to make the olive tapenade, put the olives, olive oil and capers in a blender and process to a fairly coarse mixture.

Carefully remove the skins from the peppers, making sure you don't tear the flesh, then cut each half in half again. Put each piece of pepper, skinned side down, on a work surface, then smear generously with the tapenade. Add a small piece of goats' cheese and a few basil leaves. Carefully roll up the filled pepper, then put seam side down on a serving platter. Secure with a sprig of rosemary, if using, then serve.

COOK'S TIPS

Don't overfill the peppers – any remaining tapenade can be put in a screw-top jar, covered with a thin layer of olive oil and stored in the refrigerator for 2–3 weeks.

The rosemary skewers not only look good, but they also flavour the peppers.

4 red peppers, halved, deseeded and white membranes removed

olive oil, for sprinkling

150 g goats' cheese, soft or firm, but not hard

a handful of fresh basil leaves

sprigs of rosemary, to serve (optional)

OLIVE TAPENADE

175 g black olives, pitted

4 tablespoons olive oil

2 tablespoons capers, rinsed and drained

a baking tray

MAKES 16

aubergine party rolls
filled with mozzarella and sun-dried tomatoes

These rolls look beautiful as part of a fingerfood selection. The real delight is that the flavour improves if they are made the day before – which, of course, leaves you free to concentrate on other things. Make plenty, since they will be devoured very quickly.

2 medium aubergines, cut into about 18 thin slices

olive oil, for brushing

sea salt

½ jar of basil pesto (not all of this will be used)

50 g sun-dried tomatoes, soaked overnight in warm water with 1 tablespoon vinegar, then sliced into strips

100 g mozzarella cheese, cut into small strips

salad leaves such as rocket, radicchio or red endive, to serve

a baking tray

MAKES 36

Set the aubergine slices on the baking tray, brush with olive oil, then lightly sprinkle with salt. Roast in a preheated oven at 200°C (400°F) Gas 6 for about 30 minutes or until tender. Remove from the oven and let cool slightly.

Spread each slice of aubergine with pesto. Add a slice of tomato and a strip of mozzarella. Roll up, then put seam side down on a serving platter. (The rolls look prettier if a little cheese and tomato tumbles out of the ends.)

Serve on salad leaves.

COOK'S TIP

I prefer the unhydrated variety of sun-dried tomatoes because I am outraged by the exorbitant prices of those packed in oil. It is so easy to hydrate the tomatoes yourself and it requires just a little planning.

250 g strawberries,
stalks on

250 g cherries, stalks on

30 g milk chocolate,
broken into small pieces

30 g white chocolate,
broken into small pieces

30 g dark chocolate,
broken into small pieces

greaseproof paper

mini muffin paper cases

SERVES 4

strawberries and cherries

in tricolour chocolate

A truly seductive end to any party, these fruits make for a great finale.

Divide the strawberries and cherries into 3 equal piles.

Put the milk chocolate into a clean, dry, heatproof bowl and set over a saucepan of gently simmering water. Do not let the water touch the base of the bowl, or any water touch the chocolate, or the chocolate will seize and be unusable.

Take one of the piles of fruit and dip them halfway into the chocolate, leaving the tops and stalks uncoated and visible. Transfer to a sheet of greaseproof paper to set.

Repeat with the white and dark chocolate and the other two piles of fruit. Chill for at least 1 hour.

To serve, peel off the greaseproof paper and put a selection of fruit in a mini muffin case. Alternatively, pile the fruit onto a large serving plate and invite your guests to help themselves.

COOK'S TIP

You must use a clean, dry bowl for each kind of chocolate, or the chocolate will be spoiled.

LITTLE MEALS AND TAPAS

sesame sweet potato wedges
with peanut dipping sauce

If, like me, you love the goodness of peanuts but cannot face peanut butter, you'll really appreciate this dipping sauce. It works superbly with the sweetness of the potato, which can be either roasted or deep-fried. Wonderful served with very cold beer.

Arrange the sweet potato wedges in a single layer on the baking tray, then sprinkle with the olive and sesame oils, sesame seeds and salt. Roast in a preheated oven at 200°C (400°F) Gas 6 for 35 minutes or until tender (the cooking time will vary depending on the size of the wedges).

Meanwhile, to prepare the dipping sauce, put the peanut butter, lime juice, chilli, soy sauce and tomato ketchup in a food processor, add 4 tablespoons hot water and blend until smooth. Add salt and pepper to taste, then pour into a saucepan and heat gently.

Sprinkle the wedges with the coriander and serve with a separate bowl of the dipping sauce.

COOK'S TIP

To simplify this recipe even further, serve the wedges with shop-bought sweet chilli sauce.

750 g sweet potatoes, well scrubbed but unpeeled, cut lengthways into thick wedges

2 tablespoons olive oil

1 tablespoon sesame oil

1 tablespoon sesame seeds

sea salt

fresh coriander, coarsely torn or chopped, to serve

DIPPING SAUCE

2 tablespoons organic peanut butter

1 tablespoon lime juice

1/2 red chilli, deseeded and sliced

1 tablespoon soy sauce

1 tablespoon tomato ketchup

sea salt and freshly ground black pepper

a baking tray

SERVES 6–8

saffron chickpeas

This is a wholly Italian recipe using ingredients that most Italians have in abundance in their kitchens. It is amazing how these few humble items are totally transformed by the scented elegance of saffron, bringing a touch of class to the dish.

2 tablespoons olive oil

1 onion, finely chopped

350 g dried chickpeas, soaked overnight, then drained and cooked for 1–1½ hours (reserve some of the cooking liquid to use in the recipe)

3 large tomatoes (about 350 g), skinned and chopped

2 garlic cloves, crushed

300 ml chickpea cooking liquid (see above)

a small pinch of saffron threads

sea salt and freshly ground black pepper

SERVES 4

Heat the oil in a large saucepan, add the onion and cook for 10 minutes until translucent. Stir in the drained chickpeas, tomatoes and garlic. Cook for 5 minutes, stirring occasionally.

Add the chickpea cooking liquid and bring to the boil, then reduce the heat and simmer for 25 minutes. Stir in the saffron and cook for a further 5 minutes. Add salt and pepper to taste, then serve.

COOK'S TIPS

Saffron is produced by drying the stigmas of certain varieties of crocus. Only 3 stigmas per flower can be harvested, making saffron an expensive spice, but worth every penny.

Dried beans are infinitely better than the canned varieties, which often have extra salt and sugar added – they are also much cheaper to buy. This recipe in particular should not be attempted with anything other than dried chickpeas, or it will be a mere shadow of the original dish.

couscous tabbouleh

One of my favourite salads. Don't be alarmed at the small quantity of couscous used – the salad is traditionally made mainly with herbs and vegetables and just a smattering of bulghar wheat. Couscous, a fine pasta from Morocco, is an easy alternative, very nutritious and light.

Put the couscous in a bowl with 250 ml cold water – enough to make the couscous just moist rather than saturated. Leave for 10 minutes or until fluffy. When ready, stir in the spring onions, cucumber, tomatoes, parsley and mint.

To make the lemon dressing, put the lemon juice, garlic and olive oil in a bowl and whisk with a fork. Stir into the salad, add salt and pepper to taste, then serve.

COOK'S TIP

I always like to use cold water to hydrate couscous, rather than using boiling water or steaming it. It still fluffs up well, but also retains an interesting al dente texture, which I much prefer.

75 g couscous

4 spring onions, finely chopped

1/3 cucumber, cut into very small cubes

3 tomatoes (about 300 g), deseeded then cut into small cubes

a large handful of fresh flat leaf parsley leaves, finely chopped (60 g)

a small handful of fresh mint leaves, finely chopped (20 g)

LEMON DRESSING

freshly squeezed juice of 1 lemon

1 garlic clove, crushed

3 tablespoons olive oil

sea salt and freshly ground black pepper

SERVES 4

olives, tomatoes and feta tapas in chilli oil

Olives, tomatoes and feta go perfectly with beer, making this one of my favourite tapas recipes. It makes more than you'll need for four people, but I find that the more glasses of beer I drink, the more I eat. Make extra and keep it in a covered bowl in the refrigerator to enjoy over several days – divine!

Remove the hard core from the tomatoes by making a V-shaped incision with a sharp knife. Put the tomatoes on the baking tray and sprinkle with salt and brown sugar. Push a slice of garlic into the soft seeds of each tomato, then roast in a preheated oven at 200°C (400°F) Gas 6 for 1 hour until quite dry.

Put the tomatoes in a serving bowl, add the olives, cheese, chilli oil, olive oil and lemon zest. Toss well, top with the basil, then serve.

250 g vine-ripened tomatoes, halved

sea salt, to taste

brown sugar, to taste

2 garlic cloves, thinly sliced

200 g green olives

200 g black olives

200 g feta cheese, cut into cubes

2 tablespoons chilli oil

2 tablespoons olive oil

grated zest of ½ unwaxed lemon

a handful of basil leaves

a baking tray

SERVES 4

smoky paprika-roasted potatoes

Smoked paprika transforms the humble baked potato into something special. Be restrained with the smoked paprika though – it is a very potent spice and should only be used in moderation.

1 teaspoon smoked paprika

4 teaspoons paprika

1 tablespoon olive oil, plus extra for sprinkling

750 g baby new potatoes

sea salt, to serve

SOUR CREAM TOPPING

a small handful of fresh dill, finely chopped

150 ml sour cream

1 garlic clove, crushed

freshly ground black pepper

a baking tray, lightly greased

SERVES 4

Put the prepared baking tray in a preheated oven at 200°C (400°F) Gas 6 for 5 minutes.

Put the smoked and regular paprika in a bowl and mix. Put the olive oil in a second bowl, add the potatoes and turn until covered with oil. Roll each potato in the paprika mixture until evenly coated. Transfer to the hot baking tray and sprinkle with olive oil. Roast for 1 hour, or until the skins are golden and starting to crisp.

Meanwhile, to make the sour cream topping, put the dill, sour cream, garlic and pepper in a bowl and mix well.

Cut a deep cross in each potato, then fill with the sour cream mixture. Sprinkle with salt and serve.

150 ml olive oil

1 red pepper, halved, deseeded and thickly sliced

1 yellow pepper, halved, deseeded and thickly sliced

550 g potatoes, thinly sliced

sea salt and freshly ground black pepper

a small bunch of flat leaf parsley, finely chopped, to serve (optional)

SERVES 4

calabrian-style potatoes and peppers

This is a fine example of the 'less is more' approach to entertaining – simple, good-quality ingredients cooked to perfection.

Heat the oil in a large, lidded frying pan. Add the red and yellow peppers and cook for 10 minutes, stirring occasionally, until starting to turn golden brown. Add the potatoes, salt and pepper to the pan, cover with a lid and cook for 5 minutes.

Remove the lid and continue cooking for 15 minutes, turning every few minutes as the potatoes begin to brown, taking care not to break them. If the potatoes start to stick, this will just add to the flavour of the dish, but don't let them burn.

When the potatoes are tender, transfer to a serving dish and top with the parsley, if using. Let cool for 5 minutes before serving.

beef tomatoes

with garlic and herb butter

To be enjoyed at their absolute best, beef tomatoes should be eaten hot and preferably in season. They make a great focal point for any meal and their lack of pretention is hugely appealing.

4 beef tomatoes

3 garlic cloves, crushed

70 g butter, softened

1 teaspoon chilli oil

a large handful of flat leaf parsley, finely chopped

freshly ground black pepper

olive oil, for sprinkling

a baking tray

SERVES 4

Remove the stalk from each tomato and carefully cut out a small cavity for the filling.

Put the garlic, butter, chilli oil, parsley and pepper in a bowl and mix well. Fill the tomato cavities with the garlic mixture, pressing down gently as you go. Put on the baking tray, sprinkle with olive oil and roast in a preheated oven at 150°C (300°F) Gas 2 for 1 hour 20 minutes.

Eat hot from the oven with some of the cooking juices poured over the top.

green beans in tomato sauce

I really love the Italian tradition of bequeathing recipes to loved ones so that they can keep the heritage and spirit of the dish alive. This recipe and those on pages 38 and 45 have been passed unchanged down five generations. They have been very kindly shared by Gabi Matzeu, as enthusiastic an Italian chef as you will find. Good served hot or cold, this is stunning in its simplicity – no antipasti selection could be complete without it.

Put the olive and chilli oils and garlic in a large saucepan and heat until the garlic has turned very lightly golden. Stir in the tomatoes, 250 ml water and a generous pinch of salt. Bring to the boil, then add the beans. Cover with a lid and cook gently for 30–40 minutes, stirring occasionally, until the beans are very tender.

COOK'S TIP

In Italy, it is a widely held belief that tomato seeds eaten in excess are bad for the liver. Thus, even simple canned tomatoes are passed through a mouli – a hand-operated rotary device – to remove the seeds. Moulis are used extensively and are a classic kitchen utensil. They are superb for making purées, mashes and removing the skin of pulses to make them more digestible.

4 tablespoons olive oil

1 teaspoon chilli oil

1 garlic clove, crushed

800 g canned chopped tomatoes

sea salt

600 g green beans, topped

SERVES 4

garlic mushrooms
in white wine and cream

One of the delights of cooking with mushrooms, especially the chestnut variety, is that their flavour is so good you need add very few other ingredients. That said, the perfect partners for mushrooms are garlic and cream, a truly sublime combination.

Put the oil, butter and garlic in a large saucepan and heat until the butter melts. Stir in the mushrooms and cook for 5–10 minutes until softened.

Add the wine and cream and bring to the boil. Reduce the heat slightly and continue cooking until the liquid has reduced by half. Season to taste, stir in the parsley and serve.

COOK'S TIP

The best way to crush garlic is to slice it, add a pinch of salt, then crush it with a mortar and pestle. The salt draws out the juices to make a pulp.

1 tablespoon olive oil

50 g unsalted butter

3 garlic cloves, crushed

500 g chestnut mushrooms, thickly sliced

100 ml white wine

4 tablespoons double cream

sea salt and freshly ground black pepper

a bunch of flat leaf parsley, finely chopped

SERVES 4

1 large whole cauliflower, green leaves removed and reserved

2 onions, finely chopped

300 g small green pitted olives

sea salt

6 tablespoons olive oil, plus extra to serve

a small bunch of flat leaf parsley, finely chopped, to serve

SERVES 4

sardinian cauliflower with olives

A spectacular way to serve a whole creamy head of cauliflower – let your guests serve themselves, pulling out the florets. There's no fuss needed for this gloriously simple dish.

Line a large, heavy-based saucepan with the reserved outer leaves from the cauliflower. Put the cauliflower on top. Sprinkle with the onion, olives and some salt, then pour over the 6 tablespoons olive oil. Cover with a lid, set over the lowest heat and cook gently for about 40 minutes or until tender – there should be no resistance when a fork is inserted into the middle of the cauliflower.

Carefully lift the cauliflower out of the saucepan and onto a large plate – be very careful not to break it. Pile the onion and olives on top, then sprinkle with the parsley and more olive oil and serve.

COOK'S TIP

Putting the outer leaves of the cauliflower in the bottom of the saucepan prevents the vegetable from burning or discolouring as it cooks – a great way to make use of something that would ordinarily be discarded.

BUFFETS

baby aubergines
with raisins and feta

Aubergines are used extensively in the Mediterranean, but no one cooks them quite like the Greeks. In this dish, the sweetness of the raisins and the saltiness of the feta act as the perfect balance to the acidity of the aubergines and tomatoes. Some people salt aubergines and leave them for 30 minutes before cooking to draw out the bitter juices, but I don't think this is necessary. If the vegetable is firm to the touch, just go ahead and use it with no messing about. If possible, make this dish the day before – it tastes even better if you give the flavours time to develop.

Put the olive oil, onion and garlic in a large saucepan and fry gently for 10 minutes until the onion is soft. Add the turmeric, cumin, coriander, garam masala and paprika and continue to cook for a few more minutes. Stir in the tomatoes, sugar, pine nuts and raisins, then transfer to a large ovenproof dish. Using a fork, prick the aubergines a few times so the juices can escape and absorb the flavour of the sauce. Add to the tomato sauce, then season with salt and pepper.

Cover the dish with foil and bake in a preheated oven at 200°C (400°F) Gas 6 for 45 minutes. Remove the foil and continue cooking for a further 25 minutes. Let cool for 10 minutes, then sprinkle with the feta cheese and fresh mint and serve.

COOK'S TIP

The flavours of spices are intensified when lightly toasted. Fry the spices in a dry frying pan until they start to colour and release their aroma. You can grind them with a mortar and pestle, but I prefer to use a coffee grinder (kept only for grinding spices), because it gives a finer texture. It is also much faster, which is especially important if you are cooking for large numbers!

2 tablespoons olive oil

1 onion, finely chopped

3 garlic cloves, crushed

½ teaspoon ground turmeric

2 teaspoons cumin seeds, lightly toasted in a dry frying pan, then ground

3 teaspoons coriander seeds, lightly toasted in a dry frying pan, then ground

½ teaspoon garam masala

1 teaspoon paprika

800 g canned chopped tomatoes

1 tablespoon brown sugar

30 g pine nuts, toasted in a dry frying pan until golden

50 g raisins

500 g baby aubergines, left whole

sea salt and freshly ground black pepper

TO SERVE

100 g feta cheese, crumbled

chopped fresh mint

a large ovenproof dish

SERVES 6–8

roasted vegetable and ricotta loaf

This looks splendid displayed whole before being sliced. The cross-section looks good, too – a vision of colourful vegetables interwoven with creamy ricotta. It keeps well in the refrigerator for a couple of days.

Put the slices of aubergine on a baking tray, brush with olive oil and sprinkle with salt and pepper. Preheat the oven to 200°C (400°F) Gas 6, then put the tray in the hottest part of the oven and roast for 20–25 minutes until the aubergine is tender. Put the red and yellow peppers and courgettes on the other baking tray, sprinkle with salt, and roast for about 20 minutes or until the peppers begin to blister and the courgettes are tender.

While all the vegetables are roasting, mix the ricotta with the lemon juice, garlic, parsley, chilli, salt and pepper.

When the aubergines are cooked, add the vinegar. Put a damp cloth or clingfilm over the peppers and set aside for 5–10 minutes (this makes the skins steam off and you can peel them more easily). Cut each pepper piece in half again.

Line the loaf tin with clingfilm, then gently press slices of aubergine over the base and sides of the tin. Reserve 4 slices for the top. Spread generously with some of the ricotta mixture, then add a layer of yellow pepper, taking it up the sides of the tin if you can. Sprinkle with some of the basil, then spread with more ricotta mixture. Layer the red pepper next, followed by courgette, adding a layer of the ricotta and basil after each vegetable. Top with the reserved aubergine slices. Cover the top with clingfilm and put a weight on top. Leave overnight in the refrigerator.

Invert the loaf onto a plate and carefully pull away the clingfilm. Using a serrated knife, cut into thick slices, then serve.

2 aubergines, cut lengthways into about 5 slices

olive oil, for brushing

1 red pepper, halved and deseeded

1 yellow pepper, halved and deseeded

2 courgettes, sliced lengthways

250 g ricotta cheese

2 tablespoons lemon juice

1 garlic clove, crushed

a large handful of flat leaf parsley, finely chopped

1 red chilli, deseeded and finely chopped

1 tablespoon balsamic vinegar

a large handful of basil leaves, torn

sea salt and freshly ground black pepper

2 large baking trays

a loaf tin, 900 g

SERVES 6–8

stuffed focaccia bread

Few things will make your guests feel more cared for than homemade bread. This superb focaccia really does not take too long to prepare, and the aroma is totally beguiling.

To make the dough, put the flour, salt and yeast in a large bowl. Stir in the olive oil and 350 ml water, then bring the dough together with your hands. Knead the dough by hand until it has a smooth, springy consistency (this should take about 10 minutes) or transfer to a machine with a dough hook attachment. Return to the bowl and lightly oil the top to prevent it from drying out. Cover with clingfilm or a damp tea towel and let rise in a warm place for 30 minutes until doubled in size.

Meanwhile, to prepare the filling, put the peppers and onion in a roasting tin, sprinkle with olive oil and salt and roast in a preheated oven at 180°C (350°F) Gas 4 for 15 minutes. Remove from the oven and let cool. Transfer to a bowl, add the mozzarella, basil, tomatoes, oil, olives, salt and pepper and mix well.

When the dough has risen to double its original size, transfer to a lightly floured surface and cut in half. Roll out the first half to the size of the baking tray and use to line the tray. Spread the filling over the top, leaving a 2.5 cm border around the edge. Roll out the remaining dough and put on top of the filling. Press the edges of the dough together to seal.

Brush with the 2 teaspoons olive oil, sprinkle with sea salt and dot with sprigs of rosemary, then let rise for a further 30 minutes. Just before cooking, use your thumb to make lots of indentations in the dough – this looks very attractive when cooked. Bake in a preheated oven at 180°C (350°F) Gas 4 for 40 minutes until lightly golden.

COOK'S TIP

Try to time your cooking so that your guests are greeted by the aroma of freshly baked bread – and there will much excitement all round.

500 g strong white bread flour

1 teaspoon salt

7 g sachet easy-blend dried yeast

1 tablespoon olive oil

FILLING

1/2 red pepper, halved, deseeded and sliced

1/2 orange pepper, halved, deseeded and sliced

1 red onion, sliced

olive oil, for roasting

200 g mozzarella cheese, cut into cubes

a large handful of fresh basil, chopped

8 sun-dried tomatoes in oil, sliced

1 tablespoon oil from the jar of tomatoes

a handful of pitted black olives

sea salt and freshly ground black pepper

TO FINISH

2 teaspoons extra virgin olive oil

sea salt

small sprigs of rosemary

a baking tray, lightly greased and floured

SERVES 6–8

spinach and blue cheese filo pastries

with apricots and pine nuts

These pastries offer a lovely array of tastes and textures –
the spinach provides a neutral backdrop for the rich
cheese, sweet fruit and crunchy pine nuts, all
wrapped up in a crisp filo shell. They make quite
a sensation – and also freeze superbly.

1 tablespoon olive oil

325 g spinach, washed well

½ teaspoon freshly grated nutmeg

1 garlic clove, crushed

a small handful of fresh dill, coarsely chopped

150 g blue cheese, such as dolcelatte, cut into small cubes

70 g dried apricots, about 3–4, soaked overnight, drained and sliced

40 g pine nuts, toasted in a dry frying pan until golden

200 g filo pastry

olive oil or melted butter, for brushing

crisp salad leaves, to serve (optional)

sea salt and freshly ground black pepper

a baking tray, lightly oiled

MAKES 6 ROLLS

Heat the oil in a wok or frying pan over medium heat. Add the spinach, nutmeg and garlic and stir-fry until the spinach has just wilted. Drain through a colander and let cool, then squeeze out the liquid with the back of a spoon. Put the spinach mixture in a bowl and add the dill, blue cheese, apricots, pine nuts, and salt and pepper to taste.

Cut 2 sheets of the filo pastry to about 30 x 15 cm. Put 1 sheet on a work surface and brush with oil or melted butter. Put the second sheet on top. Divide the filling into 6 portions. Spoon 1 portion along the narrow edge and firmly roll up the double layer of pastry, tucking in the ends as you go. Repeat until all the filling has been used and you have 6 rolls.

Transfer to the prepared baking sheet and bake in a preheated oven at 180°C (350°F) Gas 4 for 25 minutes, then turn over and cook for a further 15 minutes. Serve 1 roll per person, with a few crisp salad leaves, if using.

trottole pasta salad with peppers and garlic

I try to avoid using pasta because it seems to have become so synonymous with vegetarian dining. However, for a buffet I think pasta is a great idea – it really does appeal to everybody. This recipe lends itself to a large occasion because the vegetables and bread can be prepared in advance, then left overnight to soak up the flavours of the olive oil, garlic and vinegar. As the guests are due, toss in the pasta, basil, salt and pepper.

Put the tomato, peppers, bread and garlic in a large bowl with the olive oil and vinegar. Leave for a couple of hours or overnight to develop the flavours.

Cook the pasta according to the instructions on the packet. Cool with cold water, then mix into the vegetables with the basil. Season to taste and serve.

1 beef tomato, cut into tiny cubes

$1/2$ red pepper, halved, deseeded, then cut into tiny squares

$1/2$ yellow pepper, halved, deseeded, then cut into tiny squares

$1/2$ orange pepper, halved, deseeded, then cut into tiny squares

100 g ciabatta bread, cut into tiny pieces (stale bread also works well)

2 garlic cloves, crushed

200 ml good quality extra virgin olive oil

2 tablespoons balsamic vinegar

400 g spiral pasta, such as trottole or fusilli

a large bunch of basil leaves, coarsely chopped

salt and freshly ground black pepper

SERVES 6–8

nectarine and raspberry tart

with vanilla cream

This is a sumptuous-looking pudding that isn't too calorific! For a variation on the theme, try using peaches, blueberries and blackberries with redcurrants scattered over the top.

To make the vanilla cream, put the milk and vanilla pod in a medium saucepan and bring to the boil. Put the egg yolks, sugar and cornflour in a separate bowl. Using an electric beater, whisk until pale and creamy, then mix in the hot milk. Reduce the heat to low, then return the mixture to the pan, stirring constantly until it has thickened. Remove the pod, then stir in the melted butter. Transfer to a bowl, cover with clingfilm or greaseproof paper to prevent a skin from forming, then let cool.

To make the tart, roll out the pastry and use it to line the baking tray. Pour the vanilla cream over the top leaving a 2.5 cm border around the edge. Arrange alternate slices of nectarines and plums on top of the cream. Brush the exposed pastry with melted butter. Sprinkle the brown sugar over the fruit and cook in a preheated oven at 200°C (400°F) Gas 6 for 25 minutes until golden.

Serve with the fresh raspberries scattered over the top and a dusting of icing sugar.

COOK'S TIP

To make vanilla sugar, break a couple of vanilla pods in half and put in a jar with a lid. Pour the caster sugar on top. Use the next day and keep refilling with more sugar. When you remove the lid, you're assailed with a divine vanilla fragrance.

VANILLA CREAM

325 ml milk

1 vanilla pod, split in half lengthways

4 egg yolks

65 g vanilla sugar or caster sugar

2 tablespoons cornflour

25 g unsalted butter, melted

FRUIT TART

375 g puff pastry

3 nectarines, thinly sliced

3 plums, sliced (yellow plums look very pretty)

melted butter, for brushing

½ tablespoon brown sugar

150 g raspberries

icing sugar, for dusting

a baking tray, 30 x 23 cm

SERVES 6–8

SPONGE CAKE

225 g unsalted butter, softened

225 g caster sugar

4 large eggs, lightly beaten

50 g plain flour

275 g ground almonds

MINT SYRUP

30 g caster sugar

12 fresh mint leaves, finely chopped

TRIFLE FILLING

about 500 g mascarpone cheese

25 g caster sugar

3 egg yolks

250 g raspberries

250 g strawberries

a small handful of fresh mint leaves

a cake tin, 20 cm diameter, lined with greaseproof paper

SERVES 6

strawberry and mascarpone trifle

This extraordinarily versatile pudding is perfect for a warm, lazy day. Red fruit always looks magnificent but you could also use blueberries, mangoes and passionfruit. Only about half of the sponge is necessary for this trifle, so freeze the rest for an extra-speedy version next time round. The sponge has a dense, chewy texture to absorb the mint syrup. The mint is a perfect partner for the strawberries, but you could also use fruit juice or sweet wine.

To make the sponge cake, put the butter and sugar in a medium bowl and beat with an electric beater until the mixture is pale and creamy. Slowly add the eggs, beating well between each addition. Using a metal spoon, fold in the flour and ground almonds.

Spoon into the prepared cake tin and bake in the centre of a preheated oven at 180°C (350°F) Gas 4 for 40 minutes until springy to the touch or until a skewer can be removed cleanly when inserted into the middle.

To make the mint syrup, put the sugar, mint and 75 ml water in a small saucepan. Bring to the boil and continue to boil until reduced by one-third.

To make the filling, put the mascarpone, sugar and egg yolks in a bowl. Using an electric beater, beat the mixture until creamy. Using a fork, lightly mash the raspberries to a purée. Chop half the strawberries into small pieces, and cut the remainder in half, leaving the stalks intact for decoration.

To assemble the trifle, break the cake into large pieces and put into a large dish or 6 individual dishes. Moisten the cake with the mint syrup and add some of the mint leaves. Spoon in the raspberry purée, then the chopped strawberries, then the mascarpone. Top with the strawberry halves, then chill in the refrigerator for at least 1 hour before serving.

CASUAL LUNCHES

buckwheat noodles in miso ginger broth

This dish is a meal in itself and incredibly versatile. Mushrooms, mangetout, broccoli, baby corn or Chinese leaf all work well – use whatever is in season, or more to the point, what's in the refrigerator! The same applies to the noodles. I like buckwheat noodles because they thicken the dish slightly and have a gorgeous nutty flavour. Use your favourite – the choice is endless with both fresh and dried noodles.

Cook the noodles according to the packet instructions, then rinse well.

Put the sesame and sunflower oils, onion, chilli, ginger and soy sauce in a large saucepan. Cook gently for 10 minutes until the onion is soft, then stir in the stock and beans. Bring gently to the boil, then add the carrots and oyster mushrooms. Continue cooking for 2–3 minutes, then add the bok choy and cooked noodles. Again, continue simmering for 1–2 minutes. Add the miso, enoki mushrooms, beansprouts and spring onions, then serve immediately while the vegetables are still crunchy and vibrant in colour.

COOK'S TIPS

Miso is a fermented paste of soya beans. There are various types depending on the culture used to ferment the beans – barley, rice and wheat are all available. The miso is stirred in at the end of the cooking process so that its nutritional content is not diminished.

Enoki mushrooms are small mushrooms with long stems and tiny white caps. They are usually bought in clumps with the root base still attached – this is removed before cooking.

If you are using fresh noodles, there is no need to precook them. Simply stir them in with the bok choy.

175 g buckwheat noodles

1 teaspoon sesame oil

1 tablespoon sunflower oil

1 red onion, finely chopped

1 red chilli, deseeded and finely chopped

3 cm fresh ginger, peeled and grated

4 tablespoons soy sauce

1 litre vegetable stock

150 g green beans, topped

150 g carrots, cut into matchsticks

125 g oyster mushrooms, thickly sliced

225 g bok choy, cut into thick rounds

3 tablespoons miso paste

100 g enoki mushrooms, root base removed

150 g beansprouts, rinsed and drained

7 spring onions, cut lengthways into strips

SERVES 4

POLENTA ROUNDS

50 g unsalted butter

1 tablespoon olive oil

1 garlic clove, crushed

900 ml vegetable stock

100 g polenta

8 spring onions, thinly sliced

100 g spinach, thinly sliced

sea salt and freshly ground black pepper

250 g mozzarella cheese, sliced

ROASTED VEGETABLES

800 g butternut squash, peeled, cut in half with seeds removed

1 red ramiro pepper, halved and deseeded (long pepper)

1 yellow ramiro pepper, halved and deseeded (long pepper)

2 red onions, cut into wedges

1 whole head of garlic, cloves separated but skins left on

4 heads of baby fennel, quartered, or 2 medium heads of fennel, thickly sliced

a handful of thyme sprigs, stalks left on

a handful of oregano sprigs, stalks left on

2 sprigs of fresh rosemary

4 tablespoons olive oil

250 g mini plum or cherry tomatoes

15 asparagus spears

4 tablespoons balsamic vinegar

sea salt and freshly ground black pepper

2 large baking trays, 35 x 23 cm

a biscuit cutter, 7.5 cm diameter

SERVES 4

spinach and mozzarella polenta
with roasted vegetables, herbs and balsamic

Roasting must be one of the simplest of all cooking techniques. It reinforces the idea that when good-quality ingredients are used, very little has to be done to them. In this recipe, roasting brings out the natural sweetness of the vegetables, which is complemented by the contrasting oaky flavour of balsamic vinegar. Include as many different-coloured vegetables as possible, cut them into different shapes and don't be tempted to cook everything at once.

To make the polenta, put the butter, oil and garlic in a medium saucepan. Cook lightly, then add the stock and bring to the boil. Pour in the polenta, whisking constantly, then add the spring onions and spinach. Add salt and pepper to taste, then continue stirring. Cook as instructed on the polenta packet – the time will vary depending on the type of polenta used. Spoon into one of the baking trays and set side for about 2 hours, or until firm to the touch.

To make the roasted vegetables, put all the vegetables, except the tomatoes and asparagus, on the second baking tray. Sprinkle with the herbs, olive oil, salt and pepper and mix well. Roast in a preheated oven at 200°C (400°F) Gas 6 for 30 minutes, then stir in the tomatoes and asparagus. Continue cooking for a further 20 minutes until all the vegetables are tender.

Invert the polenta onto a work surface and cut out 8 rounds with the biscuit cutter. Brush the baking tray with olive oil and arrange the rounds on the tray. Top each round with a slice of mozzarella and bake in the oven for 10–15 minutes.

Put 2 rounds of polenta on each plate, add the roasted vegetables, then sprinkle with 1 tablespoon balsamic vinegar. Serve immediately.

VARIATION

Try this with roasted chunks of aubergine, carrots, courgettes, patty pan squash or sweet potatoes.

gado gado salad
with hot satay sauce

This is a dish full of contrasts: a rich, hot and spicy sauce served over a cool, crunchy, fragrant salad. Fantastically healthy and well balanced, too. The sauce also freezes excellently – make extra and keep the rest for another day.

Put the potatoes in a saucepan, add a pinch of salt and water to cover, bring to the boil and simmer for 15 minutes, or until tender. Drain, let cool, cut into thick slices and transfer to a large serving bowl.

Bring another saucepan of salted water to the boil and plunge in the beans. Cook for 5 minutes until tender. Remove and cool under cold running water. Drain and add to the bowl. Using the same water, cook the carrots for 3–4 minutes until tender but retaining a little bite. Remove and cool under cold running water. Drain and add to the bowl.

Stir in the cabbage, cucumber, beansprouts and coriander.

Meanwhile, pour the sesame oil into a frying pan and heat gently. Stir in the eggs and cook for 2–3 minutes until just set. Invert the omelette onto a plate, then flip back into the pan to cook the other side for a further 2–3 minutes. Transfer to a chopping board, roll up into a cylinder, then let cool. Cut into slices when cool.

Put the peanuts on the baking tray and roast in a preheated oven at 200°C (400°F) Gas 6 for about 15 minutes or until starting to colour. Toss with the soy sauce and return to the oven for a further 5 minutes. Crush the nuts in a food processor, or by wrapping them in a tea towel and crushing with a rolling pin. Stir the nuts and omelette strips into the salad, then add salt and pepper to taste.

To make the satay sauce, put the sunflower and sesame oils, onion, chilli, garlic and ginger in a saucepan and cook gently for 10 minutes until the onion is very soft. Stir in the coconut milk, tomato ketchup, peanut butter, soy sauce, lime juice and salt and continue cooking for a further 10 minutes. Transfer to a food processor and blend until completely smooth.

Serve the salad piled high on a plate with the hot sauce poured over the top.

COOK'S TIP

This sauce is very good stirred through noodles, then topped with fresh coriander and sesame seeds. Quick and delicious.

400 g waxy potatoes

150 g green beans, topped

250 g carrots, cut into long matchsticks

300 g white cabbage, cored and thinly sliced

150 g cucumber, cut lengthways into quarters, then sliced into chunky pieces

150 g beansprouts, rinsed and drained

a big handful of fresh coriander, coarsely chopped

1 teaspoon sesame oil

4 eggs, lightly beaten

150 g raw unsalted peanuts

1 tablespoon soy sauce

sea salt and freshly ground black pepper

SATAY SAUCE

1 tablespoon sunflower oil

1 teaspoon sesame oil

1 red onion, finely chopped

1–2 red chillies, finely chopped

2 garlic cloves, crushed

3 cm fresh ginger, peeled and grated

400 ml canned coconut milk

2 tablespoons tomato ketchup

3 tablespoons organic peanut butter

1 tablespoon soy sauce

freshly squeezed juice of 1 lime

sea salt

a baking tray

SERVES 4

roasted butternut squash risotto

Butternut squash is up there as one of my all-time favourite vegetables. It's gorgeous – the best of the huge range of squashes available, with a lovely deep orange hue. Roasting heightens its sweetness, and with cream, butter or cheese makes for a fantastic harmony of flavours.

Put the squash on a baking tray and sprinkle with salt and 2 tablespoons olive oil. Roast in a preheated oven at 200°C (400°F) Gas 6 for 30 minutes until tender.

Put the butter, remaining olive oil and garlic in a medium saucepan. Cook gently for 2 minutes, then add the oregano, sage and rice. Let the rice absorb the buttery juices, then stir in a ladle of the hot stock. Wait until the stock has been absorbed, then add the wine and the rest of the stock, a ladle at a time, making sure it has been completely absorbed between each addition. Stir in the squash and lightly mash with the back of a fork, leaving some pieces whole. Stir in the lemon juice and add salt and pepper to taste.

Serve topped with a generous spoonful of mascarpone.

COOK'S TIP

The risotto is good served with a light salad of lamb's lettuce, thin slices of roasted courgette and cherry tomatoes or steamed vegetables.

1 butternut squash (about 1 kg), peeled, deseeded and cut into small cubes

4 tablespoons olive oil

40 g unsalted butter

2 garlic cloves, crushed

a handful of fresh oregano leaves, finely chopped

10 sage leaves

275 g risotto rice, such as arborio

1.25 litres hot vegetable stock

200 ml white wine

1 teaspoon lemon juice

sea salt and freshly ground black pepper

mascarpone cheese, to serve

a baking tray

SERVES 4

leek, feta and black olive tart

with endive and watercress salad and spiced walnuts

This tart can be made with a multitude of complementary toppings: onion, thyme and blue cheese; wild mushroom and goats' cheese; or spinach, ricotta and pine nuts. It is quite substantial, so take advantage of the vast array of leaves now available and serve with a tasty but light salad. I like to use the slightly bitter salad leaves because they cut through the richness of the tart very well.

LEEK TART

375 g puff pastry, thawed if frozen

1 tablespoon olive oil

400 g leeks, finely sliced

a large handful of fresh dill, coarsely chopped

200 g feta cheese, cut into small cubes

100 g pitted black olives

sea salt

a baking tin, about 30 x 20 cm

a baking tray

SERVES 4–6

Roll out the pastry to fit the tin almost exactly. Trim and discard a tiny strip around the edge of the pastry so that it will rise evenly.

Heat a wok or frying pan, add the oil and leeks and stir-fry. Add just a little salt, then stir in the dill. Transfer to a colander to drain. Cool.

Arrange the leeks over the base of the pastry. Top with the feta and olives. Bake in a preheated oven at 200°C (400°F) Gas 6 for 35 minutes, or until the pastry has risen and is golden brown.

Serve with the endive salad (right).

ENDIVE AND WATERCRESS SALAD

100 g walnuts

1 tablespoon soy sauce

1 teaspoon chilli oil

2 heads of chicory, halved lengthways

freshly squeezed juice of ½ lime

175 g watercress

1 small head of radicchio, cored and shredded

30 g dried mango, soaked overnight, then sliced into long strips

DRESSING

150 ml sour cream

1 tablespoon lemon juice

2 teaspoons truffle oil (optional)

1 garlic clove, crushed

salt and freshly ground black pepper

a baking tray

SERVES 4–6

Put the walnuts on the baking tray and roast in the centre of a preheated oven at 200°C (400°F) Gas 6 for 15 minutes or until golden and aromatic. Sprinkle with soy sauce and chilli oil, toss well, then return to the oven for a further 10 minutes. Let cool.

Cut the chicory into long strips and put in a large salad bowl. Add the lime juice and toss to prevent discoloration. Add the walnuts, watercress, radicchio and mango strips.

Mix the dressing ingredients in a small bowl and serve separately so that the colours of the salad won't be masked by the sour cream.

exotic fruit scrunch

There are no limits to this pudding, which can be made with any fruits you like. The top can be decorated as extravagantly as you dare using grated or melted chocolate, lightly toasted desiccated coconut or flaked almonds, or a purée of sieved raspberries dribbled 'Jackson Pollock style' over the top! For anyone who feels guilty about puddings, take heart – the topping includes nearly as much yoghurt as cream.

Put the flour and oats in a medium bowl and mix well. Using your fingertips, rub in the butter until the mixture resembles breadcrumbs. Stir in the brown sugar, then press the mixture firmly onto the prepared tray. Bake in a preheated oven at 200°C (400°F) Gas 6 for 15 minutes until lightly golden. Let cool, then break it up into large random-sized pieces.

To make the cream topping, whip the cream until soft peaks form. Stir in the yoghurt and icing sugar to taste.

Put the pieces of the oat scrunch in a large glass serving bowl or individual glasses, top with the papaya and mango, then the cream and yoghurt mixture and the figs. Scoop the passionfruit flesh over the top and serve.

CRISPY OAT SCRUNCH

75 g plain or brown flour

75 g whole rolled oats

50 g unsalted butter

50 g demerara sugar

CREAM TOPPING

300 ml whipping cream

200 ml Greek yoghurt

35 g icing sugar or to taste

EXOTIC FRUIT LAYERS

2 medium papayas (about 500 g), peeled, deseeded and sliced

600 g mango, peeled, deseeded and sliced (about 1 large)

2 figs, quartered

4 passionfruit, halved

a baking tray,
30 x 20 cm, oiled

SERVES 4

75 g unsalted butter, softened

200 g caster sugar

3 eggs, separated

1 teaspoon vanilla essence

750 g cream cheese

2 teaspoons cornflour

1 teaspoon baking powder

TO SERVE

a selection of summer berries, such as raspberries, redcurrants and blueberries

icing sugar, for dusting

a Swiss roll tin, 33 x 23 cm, greased and lined with baking parchment

SERVES 6

polish cheesecake
with summer berries

This rich, dense, but surprisingly light cheesecake is served in shallow slices. It works equally well served with a strong espresso or as a pudding at the end of a meal. Try it with summer berries, as here, or with rhubarb purée.

Put the butter, sugar, egg yolks and vanilla essence in a bowl. Whisk with an electric beater until the mixture is pale and creamy.

Put the egg whites in a clean, dry bowl and whisk until soft peaks form.

Using a metal spoon, very lightly stir the cream cheese, cornflour and baking powder into the butter mixture. Add the egg whites and mix lightly.

Spoon into the prepared Swiss roll tin and spread evenly with a spatula. Bake in a preheated oven at 150°C (300°) Gas 2 for 1 hour. Remove from the oven and let cool in the tin – the cake will flatten naturally.

Cut the cheesecake into 12 portions and gently ease away from the baking parchment. Very carefully remove the slices of cheesecake, taking care not to break them. Put 2 slices on each plate, top with the berries, dust with icing sugar, then serve.

FORMAL DINNERS

moroccan tagine with harissa

The two main ingredients in a tagine are usually meat and dried fruit. This vegetarian twist uses chickpeas as the protein element. It works equally well, especially when served with spicy harissa sauce and crispy couscous fritters. Harissa sauce is widely available in delicatessens if you haven't the time to make your own.

CHICKPEA TAGINE

2 tablespoons olive oil

½ red onion, thinly sliced

½ white onion, thinly sliced

1 teaspoon ground turmeric

2 teaspoons cumin seeds

2 teaspoons coriander seeds, lightly toasted in a dry frying pan and ground

1 teaspoon ground cinnamon

1 red chilli, deseeded and finely chopped

800 g canned chopped tomatoes

1 tablespoon tomato purée

50 g dried apricots, soaked overnight, drained and sliced

25 g raisins, soaked overnight

75 g black olives, pitted

1 large, floury potato, cut into wedges

250 g carrots, thickly sliced

½ small green cabbage, cored and thinly sliced

500 g chickpeas, soaked overnight, drained and cooked for 1–1½ hours until tender

a large bunch of flat leaf parsley, finely chopped

a large bunch of coriander, finely chopped

sea salt and freshly ground black pepper

SERVES 4

HARISSA SAUCE

3 large fresh red chillies

1 garlic clove

2 teaspoons coriander seeds, lightly toasted in a dry frying pan and ground

1 teaspoon cumin seeds, lightly roasted in a dry frying pan and ground

4 tablespoons olive oil

1 teaspoon tomato purée

a pinch of salt

Put the chillies in a dry frying pan and cook over gentle heat, until the skins begin to blacken and blister. Remove from the heat, let cool, then remove the seeds.

Put the chillies, garlic, coriander, cumin, olive oil, tomato purée and salt into a blender and process until smooth. Use to taste in this recipe, then keep the remainder for another occasion. (It will keep, sealed, in the refrigerator for up to 2–3 weeks.)

Heat half the oil in a large saucepan. Add the red and white onions, turmeric, cumin, coriander, cinnamon and chilli and cook gently for 10 minutes until the onions are softened and translucent. Stir in the tomatoes and tomato purée and cook for 10 minutes. Add the apricots, raisins, olives, potato and carrots. Continue cooking slowly for about 45 minutes, until the carrots are tender.

Heat the remaining oil in a wok or frying pan, add the cabbage and stir-fry until just starting to soften. Add to the saucepan, then add the cooked chickpeas and bring to the boil. Stir in the parsley and coriander and season to taste.

couscous fritters

100 g couscous

a bunch of flat leaf parsley, finely chopped

a small handful of fresh mint leaves, finely chopped

100 g feta cheese, cut into small cubes

1 teaspoon cumin seeds

1 teaspoon coriander seeds, lightly toasted in a dry frying pan and ground

½ teaspoon ground turmeric

2 tablespoons lemon juice

1 tablespoon olive oil

2 eggs, 1 lightly beaten

4 tablespoons plain flour, plus extra to coat

sea salt and freshly ground black pepper

600 g breadcrumbs, made with stale white bread

sunflower oil, for frying

MAKES 12–14

Put the couscous in a bowl and cover with 250 ml cold water. Let soak for 10 minutes, then fluff it up with a fork. Stir in the parsley, mint, feta, cumin, coriander, turmeric, lemon juice, olive oil, the whole egg, and salt and pepper. Mix well, then stir in the flour. Shape into 12–14 balls and press slightly flat.

Put the beaten egg, extra flour and breadcrumbs onto 3 separate plates. Dip the balls first in the egg, then the flour, then the breadcrumbs. Pour 1 cm oil into a frying pan and heat until a cube of bread will turn golden in 1 minute. Add the fritters in small batches, spacing them well apart in the pan, and cook for 3–4 minutes until golden on both sides. Drain on kitchen paper and keep them warm in a low oven while you cook the remainder.

Serve the fritters next to the tagine with harissa sauce sprinkled over the top.

COOK'S TIP

Chillies respond very well to roasting. I like to dry-roast them in a pan on top of the oven so that I can keep an eye on them. If chillies burn, the whole room will fill with a hot, spicy, choking aroma that takes an age to dissipate – not to be recommended!

200 g filo pastry

25 g butter, melted

PASTRY FILLING

300 g tomatoes

1 tablespoon olive oil

1 teaspoon coriander seeds

1 teaspoon cumin seeds

1 garlic clove, crushed

1/2 red chilli, deseeded and finely chopped

200 g couscous

100 g dried chickpeas, soaked in water overnight, drained and cooked for 1–1 1/2 hours

70 g dried apricots, soaked in water overnight, drained and sliced

70 g raisins, soaked in water overnight

70 g flaked almonds, lightly toasted in a dry frying pan

a handful of flat leaf parsley, finely chopped

a handful of fresh mint leaves, finely chopped

200 g feta cheese, cubed

freshly squeezed juice of 1 lemon

sea salt and freshly ground black pepper

feta and chickpea parcels
with onion and tomato chutney

For these savoury pastries I leave the spices whole so that the full experience can be enjoyed. Coupled with couscous, they give it the lift it needs. Some people are surprised by the use of fruit in a savoury dish, but it is very typical of Middle Eastern cuisine. The sweetness of the dried fruit cuts through the saltiness of the cheese and diffuses the heat from any chilli. These pastries are delicious eaten hot or cold as part of a picnic. They can also be made much smaller and served as fingerfood. Usually, I serve them with spinach wilted with a pinch of nutmeg and the grated zest of 2 lemons, together with a bowl of yoghurt spiced with chilli, turmeric, coriander and cumin, all toasted. Delicious.

RED ONION, TOMATO AND OLIVE CHUTNEY

1 red onion, finely chopped

400 g tomatoes, quartered

1 tablespoon olive oil

100 g pitted black olives, finely chopped

sea salt and freshly ground black pepper

2 baking trays

SERVES 4

To make the filling for the pastries, mix the tomatoes with the olive oil, spices, garlic and chilli. Season with salt, then transfer to a baking tray. Roast in a preheated oven at 200°C (400°F) Gas 6 for 20 minutes until they collapse in on themselves.

Meanwhile, put the couscous in a bowl, add 400 ml cold water, and let soak for 10 minutes. Fluff up with a fork, then transfer to a large bowl with the chickpeas, apricots, raisins, almonds, herbs, feta, lemon juice, salt and pepper. Stir in the roasted tomatoes and mix well.

To prepare the chutney, put the red onion and tomatoes on a baking tray, sprinkle with olive oil, then roast at 200°C (400°F) Gas 6 for 20 minutes until tender. Transfer to a bowl and stir in the olives, mixing thoroughly. Add salt and pepper to taste.

Reduce the oven to 180°C (350°F) Gas 4. Put 3 sheets of the filo pastry on a work surface, overlaying them so that they form a star shape, and brush each sheet lightly with the melted butter. (Keep the rest of the filo covered with a damp cloth to prevent it drying out.)

Divide the filling into 4 portions and put 1 portion in the middle of the top sheet of filo, then pull up all the sides, twisting and pinching so that the filling is encased and the pastry is sealed. Repeat to make 4 generously sized parcels. Bake for 20 minutes until lightly golden, then cover with foil and cook for a further 15 minutes.

Serve the filo bundles with the chutney beside, and perhaps some wilted lemon spinach and spicy yoghurt (see recipe introduction).

mushrooms in ale and cream

with parsnip rösti and haricot bean mash

This dish is guaranteed to render guests speechless with anticipation and admiration. Mushrooms are often used in vegetarian cookery – and with good reason. Their distinctive flavour and heady aroma are very appealing and, with wild mushrooms, a truly exotic dish can be created. You can use the traditional potato for the rösti if you prefer, although I like the sweetness of parsnips. Coupled with the mellow bean mash, all the flavours are easy to decipher and enjoy. Serve with steamed broccoli for a flash of colour.

30 g unsalted butter

1 tablespoon olive oil

125 g shiitake mushrooms, sliced

250 g chestnut mushrooms, sliced

100 g wild mushrooms, sliced

100 g portobello mushrooms, sliced

4 garlic cloves, crushed

1 teaspoon paprika

100 ml dark ale

200 ml double cream

1 tablespoon lemon juice

sea salt and freshly ground black pepper

fresh dill, coarsely chopped, to serve

HARICOT BEAN MASH

200 g floury potatoes, cut into chunks

200 g dried haricot beans, soaked overnight, drained and cooked for 1 hour (reserving 5 tablespoons of the cooking liquid)

2 garlic cloves, chopped

freshly squeezed juice of ½ lemon

100 ml olive oil

PARSNIP RÖSTI

750 g parsnips, grated

½ teaspoon freshly grated nutmeg

2 egg yolks, lightly beaten

2 tablespoons plain flour

60 g unsalted butter

4 tablespoons sunflower oil

sea salt and freshly ground pepper

a frying pan, 15 cm diameter

SERVES 4

To make the mashed haricot beans, cook the potatoes in a saucepan of boiling salted water for 15 minutes or until tender. Drain and keep them warm. Put the drained beans in a food processor with the potatoes and garlic. Mix the reserved bean cooking liquid, lemon juice and olive oil in a measuring jug, then, with the machine running, pour into the processor in a steady stream. Transfer the mash to a bowl and keep it warm.

To prepare the mushrooms, melt the butter and olive oil in a large frying pan. Add the 4 kinds of mushrooms, garlic and paprika, and fry gently for 5 minutes until they start to soften. Stir in the ale and cream. Continue to cook for about 10–15 minutes until the liquid has reduced by half. Stir in the lemon juice and add salt and pepper to taste.

To make the rösti, put the grated parsnip in a colander and squeeze out any surplus juices with your hands. Put in a bowl and stir in the nutmeg, egg yolks, flour, salt and pepper. Melt 15 g of the butter with 1 tablespoon of the oil in the frying pan. Divide the parsnip mixture in 4 and press 1 portion into the base of the frying pan, pushing down firmly with a wooden spoon. Cook for 4–5 minutes over medium heat until golden brown and crispy. Invert onto a plate, slide back into the pan and cook the other side for a further 4–5 minutes. Don't worry if the rösti breaks up slightly – just mould it back together with the spoon. Repeat to make another 3 rösti.

To serve, spoon a generous mound of mashed haricot beans on 4 plates, then flatten slightly. Top with a rösti, making sure a little of the mash is visible around the edges. Add the mushrooms so that they are nestled on top of the rösti. Top with dill and serve.

COOK'S TIP

Mushrooms are like sponges and soak up flavourings very easily, but if they are washed they become waterlogged and lose the capacity to absorb anything else. Therefore, always wipe mushrooms rather than rinsing them before cooking.

600 g deep-fried tofu, cut into chunks

1 tablespoon soy sauce

½ teaspoon chilli oil

2 tablespoons sunflower oil

1 tablespoon sesame oil

275 g carrots, cut into matchsticks

250 g shiitake mushrooms, thickly sliced

2 tablespoons hoisin sauce

1 tablespoon soy sauce

1 tablespoon rice vinegar

9 spring onions, cut into 3 cm strips

sea salt and freshly ground black pepper

RICE PATTIES

200 g uncooked black rice (not wild rice)

1 tablespoon soy sauce

1 teaspoon sweet chilli sauce

1 egg yolk

3 heaped tablespoons plain flour

a handful of fresh chives, thinly sliced

a handful of coriander leaves, finely chopped

sea salt and freshly ground black pepper

sunflower oil, for frying

TO FINISH

1 large bok choy, thickly sliced

fresh coriander, coarsely chopped, to serve

a baking tray

SERVES 4

tofu and shiitake mushrooms

on crispy black rice patties

Rice is a staple food in the East, but in the West we have probably been a little slow in recognizing its health benefits and have also been limited by meagre choice. However, stores now offer a huge range of rice, including black, red, scented and sticky varieties. The black rice used for these patties is wonderful and lends an unusual colour to the dish.

To make the patties, put the rice and soy sauce in a saucepan and cook according to the instructions on the rice packet. When cooked, drain through a colander and rinse until the water runs clear. Put the rice in a bowl and mash with the chilli sauce, egg yolk, flour, chives, coriander, salt and pepper. Roll into 12 balls and flatten into patties. Heat about 3 cm depth of oil in a wok. When the oil is hot, add the patties a few at a time, and cook for a few minutes on each side until crisp and golden. Drain on kitchen paper and keep them warm.

Put the tofu on the baking tray and sprinkle with soy sauce and chilli oil. Cook in a preheated oven at 200°C (400°F) Gas 6 for 20 minutes. Put the sunflower and sesame oils in a wok or frying pan and heat. Add the carrots and mushrooms and cook for a few minutes until tender, but still with some bite to them. Add the hoisin, soy, rice vinegar and about 200 ml water, and continue cooking for 2 minutes. Stir in the spring onions, roasted tofu, and salt and pepper to taste.

Using a separate wok or a large frying pan, stir-fry the bok choy for 2–3 minutes, until cooked but still a little crunchy.

Put 3 patties on each plate, with a mound of bok choy and the tofu and mushrooms spooned alongside. Sprinkle chopped coriander over the top and serve.

COOK'S TIP

I like to use deep-fried rather than plain tofu because the texture, flavour and appearance is enhanced by the frying process. Tofu is available from health food shops already fried, or it is easy to fry your own. Heat the oil and put the cubes of firm tofu in the oil until they swell up. Alternatively, the tofu could be first marinated, then deep-fried to get the maximum flavour possible.

mango and lime tart brûlée

250 g sweet shortcrust pastry

200 g caster sugar

4 eggs

250 ml double cream

200 ml mango pulp

freshly squeezed juice of 2 limes and 1 teaspoon freshly grated zest of unwaxed lime

2 tablespoons brown sugar, for sprinkling

Chantilly cream or crème fraîche, to serve

a loose-based tart tin, 30 cm diameter

baking parchment and baking beans, small weights or rice

SERVES 6–8

I'm not really a great pudding eater, but I love this one because I'm a huge fan of mango. This is an impressive-looking tart that can be rustled up effortlessly. In fact, you can make it the day before and do the 'brûlée' topping just before serving.

Roll out the pastry to fit the tin, drape it over a rolling pin, then drape the pin over the tart tin. Press the pastry into the corners, then roll the pin over the top to trim off the excess. Prick a few holes in the base, then line with baking parchment and fill with baking beans or small weights to prevent the pastry from rising. Bake in a preheated oven at 180°C (350°F) Gas 4 for 10 minutes (this is called baking blind). Gently remove the baking beans and parchment, then return to the oven to cook for a further 10 minutes or until lightly golden. Remove from the oven and let cool.

Put the sugar, eggs and cream in a bowl and beat with an electric beater. Stir in the mango pulp, lime juice and zest. Pour into the pastry case and bake for 30 minutes or until the tart is just starting to set. Remove from the oven and let cool.

Sprinkle brown sugar over the top and either put the tart under a preheated grill or use a cook's blowtorch to melt the sugar until it is molten and bubbling.

Serve with Chantilly cream or crème fraîche.

COOK'S TIP

There is no shame in using good-quality shop-bought pastry – cooking is fantastic but it is good to have a life outside as well! Fresh ready-made pastry is preferable to the frozen sort.

BARBECUES AND GRILLS

4 large portobello
mushrooms (about 250 g)

MARINADE

2 tablespoons olive oil

1 tablespoon soy sauce

grated zest and juice
of 1 unwaxed lemon

2 garlic cloves, crushed

4 sprigs of rosemary

freshly ground black
pepper

TO SERVE

crusty bread

horseradish sauce

SERVES 4

portobello mushrooms
with lemon and olive oil

The earthy, almost meaty flavour of portobello mushrooms needs very little to improve it. Simple cooking and a complement of good-quality ingredients will reveal their absolute best.

To make the marinade, put the olive oil, soy sauce, lemon zest and juice, garlic, rosemary and pepper in a bowl, mix well, then pour over the mushrooms so that they are well covered. Set aside to infuse for 30 minutes.

Put the mushrooms on the preheated barbecue or stove-top grill pan and cook for 5 minutes on each side or until softened.

Serve the mushrooms on top of crusty bread with a smear of horseradish, then pour any remaining marinade juices over the top.

aubergine and smoked cheese rolls

2 aubergines, cut lengthways into about 5 slices

1 teaspoon chilli oil

125 ml olive oil

3 teaspoons cumin seeds, lightly toasted in a dry frying pan and ground

2 garlic cloves, crushed

1 red chilli, deseeded and finely chopped

a large handful of mint leaves, finely chopped

175 g firm smoked cheese, sliced

sea salt and freshly ground black pepper

TO SERVE

a large handful of fresh coriander, coarsely chopped

freshly squeezed juice of ½ lemon

MAKES 10 ROLLS

I have a deep love affair with aubergines and have to resist the temptation to put them in everything – but it isn't easy! Truly at home in both Middle Eastern and Mediterranean cuisines, they are compatible with endless spices, herbs and a multitude of other ingredients. In this dish, they soak up the fragrance of spices and are paired with smoked cheese, enhancing the already smoky barbecue flavour.

Arrange the aubergine slices on a large tray. Mix the chilli and olive oils, cumin, garlic, chilli, mint, salt and pepper in a measuring jug, then pour over the aubergines. Turn each slice over so that both sides are well coated. Cover with clingfilm and set aside for a few hours or overnight to soak up all the flavours.

Put the aubergine on a preheated barbecue or smoking-hot stove-top grill pan. Cook for about 4 minutes, then turn and cook the other side until tender and browned.

Remove from the heat, put some of the cheese at one end of a slice of aubergine and roll up firmly (do this while the aubergine is still hot so the cheese melts). Repeat with the other slices. Sprinkle with the coriander and lemon juice, then serve.

asparagus and lemon

with smoked garlic mayonnaise

I look forward to the arrival of asparagus each year because it means that summer is just around the corner. The beauty of this vegetable is that it needs very little to go with it – just something for dunking! I believe that to roast or char-grill asparagus is to enjoy it at its best. If using a charcoal barbecue, start cooking when the coals turn white, since this is when they are at their hottest. If using a stove-top grill pan, start cooking when the pan is smoking hot to maximize the asparagus flavour.

16 asparagus spears

2–3 tablespoons olive oil

sea salt and freshly ground black pepper

freshly squeezed juice of ½ lemon, to serve

SMOKED GARLIC MAYONNAISE

3–4 smoked garlic cloves, crushed

4 tablespoons mayonnaise

SERVES 4

Heat the barbecue or stove-top grill pan.

Put the asparagus in a bowl, add the olive oil and toss to coat. Set on the hot barbecue or stove-top grill pan and cook for about 10 minutes, turning frequently, or until starting to become golden brown. Remove to a plate and sprinkle with sea salt and pepper. Squeeze the lemon juice over the top before serving.

Stir the smoked garlic into the mayonnaise and serve as the perfect accompaniment to the hot lemony fingers of asparagus.

COOK'S TIP

To prepare asparagus, just snap off and discard the woody ends (they snap naturally in the right place).

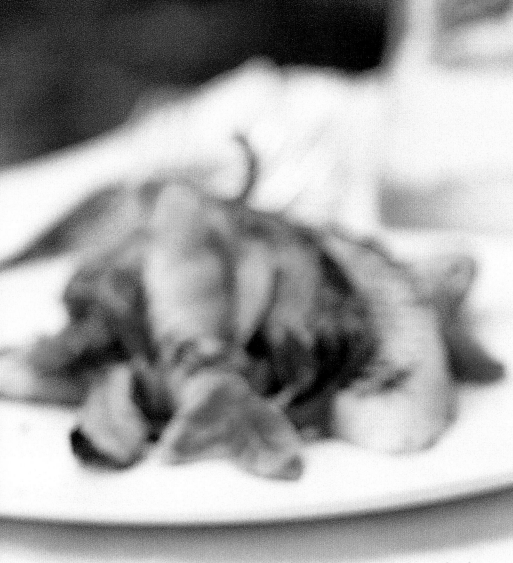

2 red ramiro peppers, halved lengthways and deseeded (long peppers)

4 slices of ciabatta bread, thickly cut diagonally

1 garlic clove

2–3 tablespoons olive oil

sea salt

torn basil leaves, to serve

SERVES 4

Put the peppers on a preheated barbecue or stove-top grill pan, then cook until the skins have blackened.

Remove the peppers, then toast the bread on both sides, taking care that it does not burn. Rub each side with the garlic clove.

Put the bread on a plate and sprinkle generously with olive oil and sea salt. Top with the pepper and basil and serve.

COOK'S TIP

Ramiro peppers are the shape of a huge chilli, but rather than being hot, they are incredibly sweet. Roasting peppers, or any vegetable for that matter, intensifies the natural sweetness – using ramiro means that you are at an advantage before you even start. They are available in red, yellow and orange and look supremely pretty served together. If you can't find them, use regular peppers.

char-grilled bread with ramiro peppers

This is a sophisticated open sandwich, with the sweetness of the roasted ramiro pepper complementing the garlicky bread. As a variation, bruschetta is always good: char the bread, rub with a raw garlic clove, sprinkle with olive oil, then squeeze half a tomato over the bread, discarding the skin. Top with slices of avocado for something a little more substantial.

250 g firm tofu

2 tablespoons hoisin sauce

3 tablespoons soy sauce

1 red chilli, finely chopped

2 cm fresh ginger, peeled and grated

1 teaspoon sesame oil

1 tablespoon rice vinegar

a handful of fresh coriander, coarsely chopped, to serve

SERVES 4

tofu in a hot, sweet and spicy infusion

Tofu receives some bad press and even I agree that it can be exceedingly dull and tasteless when served au naturel. However, it does act as a sponge for marinades. The flavours percolate all the way through, giving the tofu a fantastic extra lease of life and great versatility. For vegetarians, it is a good source of protein and, for meat-eaters, a welcome fat-free alternative.

Cut through the cake of tofu horizontally to make 2 thin slices. Cut each slice into 4 pieces.

Put the hoisin, soy sauce, chilli, ginger, sesame oil and rice vinegar in a small bowl and mix well. Pour onto a large plate, then put the tofu on top. Spoon some of the mixture over the top so that the tofu is completely covered. Leave for as long as possible to soak up the flavours, at least 2 hours or overnight.

When ready to cook, put the tofu on a preheated barbecue or smoking-hot stove-top grill pan, reserving some of the marinade. Cook each side for 4–5 minutes until lightly browned. Serve immediately with the reserved marinade, topped with coriander.

courgettes and patty pans

infused with mint and balsamic vinegar

If you think that barbecue food is predictable, this dish will change your opinion and prove to be a refreshing change. It looks and tastes sunny and fresh – you can prepare it before the guests arrive, then leave it to soak up the oil, mint and balsamic vinegar. Delicious.

Put the patty pans on a preheated barbecue or stove-top grill pan. Cook on each side for about 5 minutes or until tender, turning over when starting to char.

When cooked, transfer to a long serving dish. Pour over the oil and vinegar and sprinkle with pine nuts, mint, salt and pepper.

Cook the sliced courgettes on the barbecue or in the pan for just 1–2 minutes each side. Add to the patty pan mixture, turn to coat, cover and let marinate for about 2 hours in the refrigerator, then serve.

COOK'S TIP

Patty pans are members of the squash family and are either yellow or green. They look a little alien, rather like mini flying saucers, but taste wonderful. They are available from large supermarkets all summer.

400 g yellow and green patty pans, cut in half

6 tablespoons olive oil

2 tablespoons balsamic vinegar

40 g pine nuts, lightly toasted in a dry frying pan

a handful of fresh mint leaves, coarsely chopped

3 courgettes (about 500 g), cut lengthways into 5 mm slices

sea salt and freshly ground black pepper

SERVES 4

tuscan bread salad

The success of this simple and authentic Italian recipe depends on the finest quality olive oil. It will largely dictate the aroma and flavour of the salad. Use it generously, and don't worry about the calories – olive oil is a completely natural food, rich in the antioxidants and vitamins that help prevent body cells ageing. How many other foods can boast that!

Put the bread in a large bowl and mix in the oil, vinegar, lemon juice, garlic and 2 tablespoons water, mashing the bread a little with a fork as you go. Stir in the tomatoes, cucumber, onion, capers and basil. Season with salt and pepper and serve.

COOK'S TIP

The salad can be made in advance but must be eaten on the same day. Add the basil just before serving to keep its vibrant colour.

200 g ciabatta bread, cut into very small cubes

7 tablespoons extra virgin olive oil

2 tablespoons sherry vinegar (or use balsamic or red wine vinegar)

1 tablespoon lemon juice

1 garlic clove, crushed

2 beef tomatoes (about 300 g), cut into tiny cubes

1/2 cucumber, halved, deseeded and cut into small squares

1 red onion, finely chopped

180 g capers or caperberries

a large bunch of fresh basil leaves, torn

sea salt and freshly ground black pepper

SERVES 4

plantain with lime and chilli

Plantain lends itself very well to barbecues and grill pans. The cooking process brings out its sweetness, so it's good to offset that with a bit of citrus and chilli. It always amazes me that some people are unfamiliar with this gorgeous vegetable, which is readily available from some supermarkets or speciality Caribbean shops. It is also great shallow-fried with sweet chilli sauce served on the side.

2 plantains, thinly sliced diagonally

freshly squeezed juice of 1 lime

1 tablespoon chilli oil

sea salt

fresh coriander, coarsely chopped, to serve

SERVES 4

Put the slices of plantain in a large bowl with the lime juice and chilli oil. Carefully turn them over to cover evenly (this will stop them discolouring).

Arrange the slices on a preheated barbecue or stove-top grill pan and cook for 2–3 minutes or until slightly charred. Gently turn them over, using a palette knife, then cook the other side for 2 minutes. (The plantain changes from a fleshy colour to a beautiful bright yellow blackened with the stripes of the pan or barbecue.)

When cooked, lift onto a plate, sprinkle with salt and fresh coriander, then serve.

COOK'S TIP

When plantains are ripe and at their best for cooking, they have blackened skins and look like ordinary bananas that have gone past their best.

DILL POLENTA

30 g unsalted butter

1 tablespoon olive oil

200 g polenta

30 g Parmesan cheese, grated

20 g fresh dill, coarsely chopped

sea salt and freshly ground black pepper

MARINATED FENNEL

2 tablespoons sherry or red wine vinegar

3 tablespoons olive oil

2 garlic cloves, crushed

2 bulbs of fennel, tough outer leaves removed, remainder sliced

sea salt and freshly ground black pepper

MARINATED SPRING ONIONS

8 spring onions

1 tablespoon sherry or red wine vinegar

1 tablespoon olive oil

sea salt and freshly ground black pepper

TO SERVE

30 g Parmesan cheese, grated

grated zest of $^1/_2$ unwaxed lemon

sea salt

a Swiss roll tin, 33 x 23 cm, lightly greased

a biscuit cutter, 9 cm diameter

SERVES 4

lemon, fennel and spring onions
on char-grilled dill polenta

There are three ingredients I think fennel should never be without – lemon, olive oil and dill. If you don't have any fresh dill, chop up the feathery fronds from the top of the fennel and use instead. The polenta is used instead of bread and provides a good base for the flavours of the dish.

To make the polenta, melt the butter and oil in a medium saucepan. Add 1.25 litres water and bring to the boil. Pour in the polenta in a steady stream, whisking all the time. Continue to cook according to the instructions on the packet, until the grainy texture has disappeared. Stir in the Parmesan, dill, salt and pepper. Spoon into the prepared Swiss roll tin, then let cool until firm.

To marinate the fennel, put the vinegar, oil, garlic, salt and pepper in a bowl and mix well. Add the fennel and set aside to develop the flavours.

Put the spring onions, vinegar, oil, salt and pepper in a separate bowl and set aside to marinate.

Cut out rounds of polenta with the biscuit cutter. Cook on a preheated barbecue or stove-top grill pan for 5 minutes on each side, until browned.

Add the fennel to the barbecue or pan. Cook for 5–10 minutes until charred on both sides and tender. While the fennel is cooking, add the spring onions and cook for 2–3 minutes until lightly blackened.

Serve the polenta piled high with fennel and spring onions and sprinkle with Parmesan, lemon zest and sea salt. Pour any remaining marinade juices over the top.

char-grilled pineapple

with coconut, chilli and lime ice cream

Pineapple, coconut and lime juice – are these not the flavours of a tropical heatwave? OK, so the chilli may seem a little avant-garde, but it works! The cream and coconut diffuse the heat of the chilli so that all that remains is its taste, texture and colour – providing a flash of red on white, and making a thoroughly intriguing combination.

1 pineapple, peeled, cored and cut into 3 cm slices

10 g unsalted butter (if using a grill pan)

icing sugar, to dust

COCONUT, CHILLI AND LIME ICE CREAM

250 ml canned coconut milk

250 ml double cream

75 g caster sugar

grated zest of 2 unwaxed limes and freshly squeezed juice of 1 lime

½ large red chilli, deseeded and finely chopped

SERVES 4

To make the ice cream, put the coconut milk, cream and sugar in a saucepan. Heat gently until the sugar has dissolved. Let cool, then add the lime zest, lime juice and chilli. Transfer to an ice cream maker and churn according to the manufacturer's instructions, or pour into a rigid covered container and freeze for 1½–2 hours until the ice cream has set about 3 cm from the edge. Whisk to break down the larger crystals, then return to the freezer for a further 4 hours or overnight.

Preheat the barbecue or stove-top grill pan. If using the grill pan, add the butter and melt, to prevent the pineapple from sticking. Add the pineapple and cook for 5 minutes each side, until slightly charred.

Dust the pineapple with icing sugar and serve with scoops of the ice cream.

banana parcels with chocolate and rum

Ever so slightly decadent, this is a dish to help you re-create the taste of the Caribbean in minutes. Equally good cooked outside on a barbecue in the heat of summer or made on a stove-top grill pan in the depths of winter.

4 banana leaves or aluminium foil, cut to 25 cm square

4 bananas, halved crossways

80 g dark chocolate, broken into small pieces

4 tablespoons dark rum

1 tablespoon sunflower oil (if using a pan)

whipped cream, to serve

string or raffia, soaked in water for 15 minutes

SERVES 4

Put the banana leaves on a work surface. On the first leaf, put 2 banana halves side by side. Sprinkle with one-quarter of the chocolate and 1 tablespoon rum. Fold up the sides and edges to form a square parcel. Tie with the wet string or raffia (soaking will prevent the string from burning). Repeat to make 4 parcels.

Put the parcels on a preheated barbecue or oiled, smoking-hot stove-top grill pan and cook for about 10 minutes on each side.

Snip the string and serve with whipped cream.

COOK'S TIP

Banana leaves are readily available from larger supermarkets. To make them more malleable, put on the barbecue or grill pan for 1 minute before using. Aluminium foil makes a worthy substitute.

So, it's a family meal for eight with one vegetarian. The aim is to produce delicious food but to simplify time spent in the kitchen. However, you don't want the token vegetarian to stand out as a 'special needs' guest with an isolated menu. What would be perfect is a dish which would also serve as a complement to the meat. Here are four vegetarian dishes that work very well with meat options.

SUNDAY LUNCHES **and** FAMILY DINNERS

roasted vegetable dauphinois

This rich, creamy, garlicky sauce is offset by the earthy flavours of root vegetables, plus the slightly tart and highly aromatic sage. It is incredibly straightforward to prepare, and non-vegetarians will love it just as much – it's delicious with lamb. Serve with lemon-roasted potatoes and a herby leaf salad with mustard dressing.

1 garlic clove

butter, for brushing

400 g parsnips, topped, tailed and cut into 1 cm diagonal slices

a handful of fresh sage leaves

350 g carrots, cut into 1 cm diagonal slices

350 g uncooked beetroot, scrubbed well and cut into 1 cm diagonal slices

275 ml double cream

1 tablespoon olive oil

sea salt and freshly ground black pepper

a baking dish, about 30 cm square

SERVES 4

Rub the garlic around the base and sides of the baking dish, then brush with butter. Pack overlapping slices of parsnips into the dish. Season well with salt and pepper, then add one-third of the sage leaves.

Repeat the process, first with the carrots, then the beetroot, seasoning each layer with salt and pepper and dotting with the remaining sage. Pour in the cream.

Cover the dish with foil and bake in a preheated oven at 200°C (400°F) Gas 6 for 1 hour 40 minutes. Remove the foil and lightly sprinkle the top with the olive oil. Return to the oven and continue cooking for a further 20 minutes or until the vegetables are very tender.

red onion and taleggio tart

If you want to create a self-contained package of food that can be slotted in as a replacement to meat, this tart is perfect. It can be prepared at the last minute, so it makes a good emergency standby. You can substitute rosemary and Camembert for the richer Italian Taleggio if preferred. Serve as a vegetable accompaniment for meat-eaters in the family, and as a main course for vegetarians. Ratatouille and green beans tossed in garlic and olive oil for everyone.

350 g puff pastry

1/2 tablespoon olive oil

30 g unsalted butter

3 red onions, halved lengthways, then sliced lengthways into crescents

125 ml red wine

1 tablespoon sherry vinegar

1 tablespoon brown sugar

30 g Taleggio cheese, sliced

4 tablespoons fresh thyme leaves

sea salt and freshly ground black pepper

a biscuit cutter, 12 cm diameter

a baking tray, lightly greased

SERVES 4

Roll out the pastry on a floured work surface and cut out 4 rounds using the biscuit cutter. Set them on the prepared baking tray.

Put the olive oil and 20 g of the butter in a medium saucepan and melt over low heat. Add the onions and cook slowly for 10 minutes until very soft. Stir in the red wine, sherry vinegar and brown sugar. Continue cooking for 10 minutes, then add salt and pepper to taste.

Spoon the mixture onto the pastry rounds, leaving a 3 cm border around the edges. Melt the remaining butter and use to brush the edges. Put the Taleggio on top of the onion and sprinkle with the thyme. Bake in a preheated oven at 180°C (350°F) Gas 4 for 15–20 minutes until the pastry is golden and well risen. Eat hot or cold.

butternut squash and goats' cheese layers

These layers of sweet orange squash and molten cheese provide a truly stunning focal point to any meal. Try them with slow-cooked red cabbage, juniper and chilli, plus potato mashed with spring onion on the side. A mixed leaf salad could be substituted for the mash, since the butternut squash and goats' cheese is deceptively filling. For meat-eaters in the family, this dish goes well with roast pork.

2 butternut squash

125 g firm goats' cheese, chopped

50 g breadcrumbs

4 tablespoons Greek yoghurt

a handful of fresh marjoram leaves

a handful of fresh thyme leaves

olive oil, for sprinkling

sea salt and freshly ground black pepper

paprika, to serve

a baking tray, lightly greased

SERVES 4: MAKES ABOUT 8 STACKS

Cut the long, seedless section of squash into 2 cm rings. Reserve the bulbous part for another use. Peel the rings, then cook them in boiling salted water for 10 minutes until tender. Drain.

Put the goats' cheese, breadcrumbs, yoghurt, herbs, salt and pepper in a bowl and mix.

Put 4 rounds of squash on the baking tray, top with some of the cheese mixture, then with another round of squash, finishing with some more cheese. Repeat until you have used up all the squash and cheese.

Sprinkle the top of each stack with olive oil and bake in a preheated oven at 200°C (400°F) Gas 6 for 30 minutes. Serve 2 stacks each, sprinkled with a little paprika.

toad in the hole
with red onion gravy

A true English classic – sausages baked in a light, fluffy batter – is given an extra twist with red pepper and thyme. The dish is perfect for vegetarian friends and is wonderful served with roast beef as an alternative to Yorkshire puddings. Add roast potatoes, sweet roasted parsnips and buttery stir-fried cabbage, with the red onion gravy as the final touch. What could be better?

Cook the sausages according to the instructions on the packet. When cooked, cut them in half.

To make the batter, put the flour and salt in a bowl. Make a well in the centre and add the beaten eggs. Whisk vigorously, adding the milk as you go, until the mixture is smooth. Put in the refrigerator to rest for 30 minutes.

Meanwhile, to make the gravy, put the onions in a saucepan and add the butter, oil and rosemary. Cook over low heat for 10–15 minutes, until they start to caramelize, but not brown. Stir in the flour and continue cooking over low heat for a further 2–3 minutes. Add the sugar and wine and cook for 5 minutes. Slowly stir in the stock, bring to the boil and add salt and pepper to taste. Keep the gravy over low heat until ready to serve.

Pour about 5 mm of oil into 8 of the holes in the muffin tray. Put in a preheated oven at 240°C (475°F) Gas 9 for about 10 minutes, or until the tin and oil are very hot. Spoon the batter into the holes, then put 2 sausage halves and some red pepper in each hole. Sprinkle the thyme on top.

Put the muffin trays on a baking tray and bake for 25 minutes until golden and well risen. Serve with a sprinkle of salt and a spoonful of red onion gravy.

8 vegetarian sausages

125 g plain flour

a pinch of salt

3 eggs, lightly beaten

275 ml milk

½ red pepper, halved, deseeded and thinly sliced

a few fresh thyme leaves

sea salt, to serve

sunflower oil, for cooking

RED ONION GRAVY

2 red onions, halved and thinly sliced

25 g unsalted butter

1 teaspoon olive oil

leaves from a sprig of rosemary

1 tablespoon plain flour

1 tablespoon brown sugar

250 ml red wine

500 ml vegetable stock

sea salt and freshly ground black pepper

2 muffin trays, 6 holes each, 6 cm diameter

a baking tray

SERVES 4

SUMMER ENTERTAINING

2 aubergines, cut lengthways into about 6 slices

olive oil, for brushing

RED PEPPER SAUCE

2 red peppers, halved and deseeded

1 tablespoon olive oil, plus extra for sprinkling

1 teaspoon balsamic vinegar

sea salt and freshly ground black pepper

PESTO RISOTTO

50 g unsalted butter

1 tablespoon olive oil

1 onion, finely chopped

200 g arborio rice

1 litre hot vegetable stock

2 tablespoons pesto

125 g freshly grated Parmesan cheese

sea salt and freshly ground black pepper

TO SERVE

whole basil leaves

Parmesan cheese, shaved with a vegetable peeler

2–3 baking trays

SERVES 4

aubergine rolls with pesto risotto

Sculptural, robust and unfussy, this dish radiates the freshness and brightness of good food. The three colours of deep purple, green and red offer a mouth-watering combination to enjoy. Excellent served with a simple green salad.

Arrange the slices of aubergine on a baking tray and lightly brush with olive oil (they can also be grilled or cooked in a stove-top grill pan, if you prefer). Bake in a preheated oven at 200°C (400°F) Gas 6 for 10–15 minutes until tender but not so soft that they fall apart. Transfer to a plate.

Put the peppers on the baking tray, sprinkle with olive oil and roast for 20–30 minutes until the skins have lightly blackened and the flesh is soft.

Meanwhile, to make the risotto, put the butter and oil in a wide saucepan and melt over medium heat. Add the onion and fry for 10 minutes until soft. Stir in the rice, letting it soak up all the buttery juices. Add the hot stock, a ladle at a time, stirring constantly and letting the rice absorb the liquid between additions. This will take 15–20 minutes, and the rice should be cooked but still retain a little bite. Stir in the pesto and Parmesan and add salt and pepper to taste. The rice can be cooled, or used hot.

To assemble the rolls, put a spoonful of risotto at the narrow end of each slice of aubergine. Roll up firmly and put seam side down on the baking tray. Repeat until all the ingredients have been used. Cover the tray with foil and bake for 15 minutes until the aubergine and rice are heated through.

To complete the pepper sauce, put the roasted peppers and the tablespoon of olive oil in a food processor and blend until smooth. Stir in the balsamic vinegar and add salt and pepper to taste.

To serve, put spoonfuls of the sauce on plates, add the rolls and top with whole basil leaves and shavings of Parmesan.

1 tablespoon olive oil

½ onion, finely chopped

1 green pepper, deseeded and finely chopped

½ green chilli, deseeded and finely chopped

1½ litres vegetable stock

freshly squeezed juice of 1 lime

1 avocado, halved and deseeded

a handful of fresh mint leaves

sea salt and freshly ground black pepper

TO SERVE

Greek yoghurt

crushed ice

SERVES 4

Put the oil, onion, green pepper and chilli in a saucepan and cook over gentle heat for about 20 minutes until completely soft. Let cool.

Transfer to a blender, add the vegetable stock, lime juice, avocado flesh and mint leaves, and purée until smooth. Add salt and pepper to taste, then serve in bowls or glasses, topped with a spoonful of yoghurt and some crushed ice.

I think there's nothing better than a cold soup on a hot summer's day! The secret is to make it look gorgeous while keeping the portions small. Glasses are a great idea for serving, showing off the vibrant green colour – utterly seductive.

chilled avocado and pepper soup

150 g sugar snap peas

200 g green beans, topped

200 g feta cheese, cut into small squares

½ cucumber, halved lengthways, deseeded, then sliced diagonally

a handful of fresh mint leaves, finely chopped

1 red chilli, deseeded and finely chopped

sea salt

feta salad with sugar snaps

and minty yoghurt dressing

YOGHURT DRESSING

3 tablespoons Greek yoghurt

1 tablespoon olive oil

1 tablespoon lemon juice

SERVES 4

I really enjoy the balance of flavours and sensations in this salad. The heat of the chilli, the cool of the yoghurt and cucumber together with the saltiness of the feta make it just perfect for summer dining.

Bring a large saucepan of salted water to the boil, plunge in the sugar snaps and cook briefly until they turn bright green, about 30 seconds. Remove with a slotted spoon and transfer to a bowl of cold water.

Return to the boil, then add the beans and cook for 4 minutes until tender. Drain in a colander and refresh under cold running water.

To make the dressing, put the yoghurt, olive oil and lemon juice in a small bowl and whisk well.

Put the feta in a large bowl, add the sugar snaps, beans, cucumber and mint. Pour the dressing over the salad, toss well, then serve topped with the chilli.

I like nothing better than eating good bread with a dip and my favourite vegetable – aubergine. Give yourself plenty of time to make the bread. And try to time the last batch of baking so that the aromas leave your guests in no doubt that the bread is homemade. Serve with a salad of tomato, red onion and herbs.

coriander flatbreads
with spiced aubergines and split pea dip

CORIANDER FLATBREADS

750 g strong white bread flour, plus extra for dusting

7 g sachet easy-blend dried yeast

2 teaspoons salt

1 tablespoon cumin seeds, lightly toasted in a dry frying pan

a large handful of fresh coriander, chopped

1 red chilli, deseeded and finely chopped

about 1 litre tepid water

olive oil, for brushing

SPICED AUBERGINE

freshly squeezed juice of 1 lemon

1 red chilli, deseeded and chopped

a large handful of fresh mint leaves, finely chopped

100 ml olive oil

3 aubergines, cut into chunks

1 red onion, cut into wedges

flat leaf parsley

sea salt and freshly ground black pepper

SPLIT PEA DIP

300 g yellow split peas

1 teaspoon salt

1 teaspoon cumin seeds, lightly toasted in a dry frying pan, then ground in a coffee grinder

freshly squeezed juice of 1 lemon

2 garlic cloves, crushed

4 tablespoons olive oil, plus extra to serve

fresh dill, coarsely chopped

sea salt and freshly ground black pepper

1–2 large baking trays, lightly greased

SERVES 4

To make the flatbreads, put the flour in a large bowl, then stir in the yeast, salt, cumin seeds, coriander and chilli. Make a well in the centre and add the water. Mix with your hands to form a dough. Either transfer to an electric mixer fitted with a dough hook or continue kneading by hand for about 10 minutes or until the dough is smooth and springy to the touch. Return to the bowl, lightly brush the top with oil, then cover with clingfilm. Let rise in a warm place for 30–40 minutes.

To make the spiced aubergine, put the lemon juice, chilli, mint, olive oil, salt and pepper in a blender and process until smooth. Put the aubergines and red onions on the baking tray. Pour the olive oil mixture over the vegetables and massage in well with your hands. Bake in a preheated oven at 200°C (400°F) Gas 6 for 30 minutes, then transfer to a serving bowl and top with the parsley.

To make the dip, put the yellow split peas in a medium saucepan, then cover with cold water and add the salt. Bring to the boil and cook for 30–40 minutes until soft. Drain, then transfer to a food processor. Add the cumin, lemon juice, garlic and olive oil and blend to a smooth purée. Add salt and pepper to taste, then transfer to a bowl and sprinkle with extra olive oil and some dill.

Meanwhile, to cook the flatbreads, transfer the dough to a lightly floured work surface and knead for a few minutes. Divide into 20–25 balls. Using a rolling pin, roll the dough balls into thin, flat ovals. Put on a lightly greased baking tray and cook in batches in a preheated oven at 230°C (450°F) Gas 8 for 15–20 minutes until golden and puffy.

Serve the flatbreads with the spiced aubergine and dip.

summer brioche pudding

4 small individual brioches

500 g fresh or frozen and thawed summer berries

4 tablespoons caster sugar

clotted cream or thick whipped cream, to serve

SERVES 4

This superb pudding doesn't really have to be eaten solely in summer. I have used a bag of frozen berries, which works just as well as the fresh fruit, so this delicious recipe can be enjoyed all year round.

Carefully trim the tops off the brioches and reserve as the lids. Using a small sharp knife, cut out a large cavity in the middle of each brioche.

Put the fruit and sugar in a saucepan and heat gently until the sugar has dissolved. Dip the brioche lids into the liquid, then start spooning the fruit into the cavity. (It looks like a lot but the brioche will soak up all the fruit and juices.) Put the lids on top at a jaunty angle and chill in the refrigerator for at least 3 hours.

Serve with cream.

pan-grilled strawberries

with black pepper ice cream

Strawberries and black pepper is an unusual but famous food combination that really works. Strawberries with ice cream is also a match made in heaven, so why not combine the two ideas? I think it's fabulous and certainly proves to be a great topic for discussion among guests. The slight heat from the pepper hits the taste-buds last and marries beautifully with the sweet fruit.

10 g unsalted butter

250 g strawberries, left whole with green stalks

icing sugar, for sprinkling

PEPPER ICE CREAM

100 g caster sugar

125 g mascarpone cheese

125 g Greek yoghurt

2 level teaspoons freshly ground black pepper

an ice cream maker or freezer-proof container

SERVES 4

To make the ice cream, put the sugar and 250 ml water in a small saucepan and set over gentle heat until the sugar has dissolved. Let cool. Put the mascarpone, yoghurt and black pepper in a bowl and beat well. Using a hand whisk, beat the creamy mixture into the cooled sweet liquid.

Transfer to an ice cream maker and continue according to the manufacturer's instructions. Alternatively, transfer into a rigid container and freeze for 1$\frac{1}{2}$–2 hours, or until the mixture has set about 3 cm from the edge. Whisk to break down the larger crystals, then return to the freezer for 4 hours or overnight. Remove from the freezer 15 minutes before serving to soften.

To cook the strawberries, heat a stove-top grill pan until smoking hot. Add the butter and, when melted, add the strawberries. Press lightly onto the pan so they are branded with black lines. Turn them over and do the same on the other side. Serve immediately, dusted with icing sugar accompanied by a scoop of black pepper ice cream.

COOK'S TIP

Do not overcook the strawberries – the idea is that they remain firm with only the outsides slightly softened by the heat.

WINTER ENTERTAINING

italian borlotti beans and spelt

Borlotti beans are one of Italy's most popular beans, plump and speckled with magenta and grey. When cooked, they become creamy and slightly nutty in flavour, and serve as the perfect partner to the chewy textured spelt, which is often referred to simply as *farro*.

This dish, inspired by Gabi Matzeu, is a substantial meal – a comforting winter recipe and highly nutritious. All it needs as a partner is a leafy salad or lightly steamed greens.

3 tablespoons olive oil

3 carrots, cut into small cubes

3 celery stalks, very finely chopped

1 large onion, finely chopped

2 garlic cloves, crushed

300 g borlotti beans, soaked overnight, drained, then cooked for 1–1½ hours until tender (reserving 400 ml of the cooking liquid)

250 g organic spelt

1 litre vegetable stock

sea salt and freshly ground black pepper

shavings of fresh Parmesan cheese, to serve

SERVES 4

Put the olive oil, carrots, celery, onion and garlic in a saucepan and cook gently until soft. Press the beans and reserved bean liquor through a mouli or sieve into the vegetable mixture. This removes the bean skins, giving a smoother consistency and making the beans more digestible. Alternatively, transfer to a food processor and blend to a coarse purée.

Stir in the spelt and stock, cover with a lid and cook gently for about 1 hour, stirring frequently, until thickened (the longer the cooking time the thicker the consistency). Season to taste and serve topped with shaved Parmesan.

thyme and red onion soup

with goats' cheese croutons

There is something about the sweetness of red onions contrasting with the slight tartness of goats' cheese that proves irresistible every time. The soup can be served as a meal in itself for lunch or as a substantial first course for dinner.

Put the olive oil, onions and thyme in a large saucepan. Cook over gentle heat for about 15 minutes until the onion is very soft. Stir in the stock, red wine, sugar and vinegar. Bring just to the boiling point – but do not let it boil.

Meanwhile, put the bread under the griller. Toast 1 side, then put the cheese on the untoasted side and grill until melting.

Mix the cornflour with 1 tablespoon water to form a paste. Slowly add to the soup, stirring all the time, until glossy and thickened. Season with salt and pepper.

Serve the soup hot with a cheese crouton floating in each bowl.

VARIATION

Serve crusty bread on the side and crumble the goats' cheese over the soup.

2 tablespoons olive oil

3 red onions, quartered then very finely sliced

1 tablespoon fresh thyme leaves

1.5 litres vegetable stock

200 ml red wine

2 tablespoons brown sugar

2 tablespoons balsamic vinegar

1 tablespoon cornflour

salt and freshly ground black pepper

CHEESE CROUTONS

4 slices French bread

100 g goats' cheese, cut into 4 pieces

SERVES 4

5 shallots, chopped

3 stalks of lemongrass, outer leaves removed, white bulb very thinly sliced

3 lime leaves

3 cm fresh galangal or ginger, coarsely chopped

3 cm fresh ginger, peeled and grated

freshly squeezed juice of 1 lime

400 ml canned coconut milk

1 tablespoon soy sauce

4 teaspoons tom yam paste (see Cook's Tip)

220 g canned bamboo shoots, drained

220 g canned water chestnuts, drained

1 tablespoon sunflower oil

1 large bok choy, thickly sliced

1/2 white cabbage (about 350 g), cored and thinly sliced

100 g spinach, thinly sliced

300 g beansprouts, rinsed and drained

a large handful of fresh coriander, coarsely chopped

sea salt and freshly ground black pepper

SCENTED RICE

200 g fragrant Thai rice

1/2 teaspoon ground turmeric

1 stalk of lemongrass, broken into 3 pieces

1/2 teaspoon salt

PAPAYA SALAD

100 g raw, unsalted peanuts

1 tablespoon soy sauce

3 green, unripe papaya, peeled, halved and deseeded

freshly squeezed juice of 3 limes

1 red chilli, deseeded and finely chopped

a large handful of fresh coriander, coarsely chopped

SERVES 4

thai curry with scented rice

and spicy papaya salad

This dish has beautiful and lively flavours that dance on the palate. Visually the colours are warm and tropical, so it is especially good in the depths of winter when your guests are wistfully thinking of warmer climates.

Put the shallots, lemongrass, lime leaves, galangal, ginger, lime juice and half the coconut milk in a blender. Process to a smooth paste. Transfer to a medium saucepan and add the soy sauce, tom yam paste, bamboo shoots, water chestnuts and the remaining coconut milk. Cook over gentle heat for about 20 minutes to develop the flavours.

Cook the rice with the turmeric, lemongrass and salt, according to the instructions on the packet.

To prepare the salad, spread the peanuts in a roasting tin, sprinkle with soy sauce and toast in a preheated oven at 200°C (400°F) Gas 6 for 10 minutes. Take care, because they burn easily. Remove from the oven, let cool, then crush coarsely with a mortar and pestle.

Grate or thinly slice the papaya and put in a bowl. Add the lime juice, chilli, peanuts and coriander and mix well.

To finish the curry, heat the sunflower oil in a large wok or frying pan. When hot, add the bok choy and white cabbage and stir-fry for 3–4 minutes until starting to soften. Add the spinach, beansprouts and coriander. Cook for 1 minute until the spinach has wilted. Add the curry sauce, with salt and pepper to taste, then reheat.

Serve the curry with the rice and salad alongside.

COOK'S TIP

Thai ingredients are readily available in fresh or dried form from supermarkets and speciality shops. Lemongrass, galangal, ginger and lime leaves all freeze well if you want to keep some on hand.

butternut squash and goats' cheese gratin

with warm parsnip and ginger purée

A lovely dish, beautifully balanced and perfect for an evening at home with friends. Parsnips and ginger are a surprising combination but the sweetness of the parsnips and the warm flavour of the ginger are compelling and an interesting variation on the traditional mashed potato.

2 kg butternut squash or pumpkin

4 tablespoons olive oil

50 g unsalted butter, cut into pieces

350 g canned corn kernels, drained

1/2 teaspoon freshly grated nutmeg

2 garlic cloves, crushed

a few sprigs fresh thyme, leaves pulled off the stalk

sea salt and freshly ground black pepper

140 g fresh breadcrumbs

100 g firm goats' cheese, grated

PARSNIP MASH

750 g parsnips, coarsely chopped

1 tablespoon sunflower oil

1 teaspoon ground ginger

300 ml double cream

sea salt and freshly ground black pepper

watercress, to serve

2 ovenproof glass dishes

a baking tray

SERVES 4

Put the squash in an ovenproof glass dish with 1 tablespoon of the olive oil, the butter, corn, nutmeg, garlic, thyme, salt and pepper.

To make the topping, mix the breadcrumbs, goats' cheese and remaining oil in a bowl, then sprinkle over the squash. Cover with foil and bake in a preheated oven at 200°C (400°F) Gas 6 for 40 minutes. Remove the foil and cook for a further 15 minutes until golden brown on top.

To make the mash, put the parsnips on a baking tray and sprinkle with salt, sunflower oil and ginger. Roast for about 20 minutes until the parsnips are tender. Transfer to a food processor, add the cream and blend until smooth. Add salt and pepper to taste. Transfer to the second ovenproof glass dish, cover with foil and heat in the oven for 10 minutes.

Serve the gratin with the parsnip mash and a generous bunch of watercress on the side.

roasted sweet potatoes with beetroot and carrot salad

Peanuts give a creamy richness to sauces. Here, they are complemented by the sweetness of the potato and pineapple juice and offset by a zesty, brightly coloured topping. Like most spiced dishes, this will continue to develop in flavour if left overnight, so you can make it a day ahead. What could be easier?

Put the sweet potatoes on the baking tray and sprinkle with sunflower oil and salt. Roast in a preheated oven at 200°C (400°F) Gas 6 for 30 minutes or until tender.

Meanwhile, to make the sauce, put the onion, chilli, ginger, garlic and paprika in a medium saucepan. Cook over medium heat for 10 minutes until the onion is soft. Stir in the tomatoes, pineapple juice, stock, peanut butter and soy sauce and continue cooking gently for about 10–15 minutes until the sauce has thickened.

Heat a large wok or frying pan and add the spinach. Cook for 1–2 minutes until just wilted, then add the sauce and cooked sweet potatoes. Turn carefully to coat, then keep the pan warm over gentle heat.

To make the salad, put the carrot, beetroot, lime juice and soy sauce in a bowl and toss well. Serve the salad and sweet potatoes with couscous and fresh coriander.

1 kg sweet potatoes, cut into wedges

1 tablespoon sunflower oil

sea salt

250 g spinach

SPICY PEANUT SAUCE

1 red onion, thinly sliced

1 red bird's eye chilli, finely chopped

3 cm fresh ginger, peeled and grated

1 garlic clove, crushed

1 teaspoon paprika

400 g canned chopped tomatoes

200 ml pineapple juice

200 ml vegetable stock or water

230 g organic peanut butter

1 tablespoon soy sauce

BEETROOT AND CARROT SALAD

250 g carrots, grated

200 g raw beetroot, grated

4 tablespoons lime juice

1 tablespoon soy sauce

TO SERVE

300 g couscous, prepared according to the method on page 35

chopped fresh coriander

a baking tray

SERVES 4

rhubarb, ginger and banana crumble

Crumble is one of those familiar recipes that almost everyone has made at some time in their lives. My version is given a banana twist, which makes a wicked combination with rhubarb, ginger and crunchy oats in the crumble topping. Serve with crème fraîche or vanilla custard for a winning pudding.

Put the rhubarb in a medium saucepan and add the ginger, sugar and 2 tablespoons water. Bring to the boil and simmer for 7–10 minutes, until the rhubarb has softened. Transfer to a blender and process to a purée. Transfer to the prepared pie dish and top with the bananas and a sprinkling of cinnamon.

To make the topping, put the flour and butter in a bowl and, using your fingertips, rub the butter into the flour until it looks like fine breadcrumbs. Add the sugar and two-thirds of the oats. Sprinkle over the fruit mixture and top with the remaining oats. Bake in a preheated oven at 200°C (400°F) Gas 6 for 30–40 minutes.

Serve hot with crème fraîche.

500 g rhubarb, chopped

5 cm fresh ginger, peeled and grated

2 tablespoons caster sugar

7 medium bananas, thickly cut diagonally

¼ teaspoon ground cinnamon

crème fraîche, to serve

OAT TOPPING

125 g plain flour

90 g chilled unsalted butter, cut into cubes

125 g demerara sugar

50 g rolled oats

a pie dish, 25 cm diameter, lightly greased

SERVES 4

index